BOOKS
FOR THE PEOPLE

'Through the magic casement.' A study in child concentration from the former Middlesex County Library.

Thomas Kelly

Illustrations selected by Edith Kelly

BOOKS FOR THE PEOPLE

An Illustrated History of the British Public Library

ANDRE DEUTSCH

Some other titles by the same author

A HISTORY OF ADULT EDUCATION (1962, 2nd. edn. 1970)

EARLY PUBLIC LIBRARIES (1966)

A HISTORY OF PUBLIC LIBRARIES (1973)

First published 1977 by
André Deutsch Limited
105 Great Russell Street London WC1

Copyright © 1977 by Thomas and Edith Kelly
All rights reserved

Filmset and printed in Great Britain by
BAS Printers Limited,
Wallop, Hampshire

ISBN 0 233 96795 8

Contents

Preface

In presenting this illustrated narrative of the history of popular libraries in Great Britain, we should like to express our very great appreciation of the tremendous help we have received from librarians and others in gathering information and especially illustrative material. Pictures of all kinds have been made freely available for our examination, and in many instances prints and photographs have been specially made for our use. Where so many have been so helpful, it is difficult to single out individuals, but we cannot fail to acknowledge our special thanks to Mr W. A. Taylor, City Librarian of Birmingham; Mr W. Davies, Librarian of the Bradford Metropolitan District; Mr G. A. Dart, formerly City Librarian of Cardiff; Mr Alex Wilson, County Librarian of Cheshire; Mr O. S. Tomlinson, Assistant County Librarian of North Yorkshire; Mr M. V. J. Seaborne, Principal of Chester College; Mr Philip Whiteman of the College of Librarianship, Wales; and Mr H. Francis of the South Wales Miners' Library at Swansea. The British Library and the Library Association have also given quite indispensable assistance. In the British Library we have received particular help from Mr E. J. Miller of the Reference Division; Mr Maurice Line, Director-General of the Lending Division; and Mr J. C. Downing of the Bibliographic Services Division. In the Library Association we have drawn heavily on the assistance of Mr L. J. Taylor and Miss Andrea Polden in the Library (now part of the British Library) and of Mrs Kate Wood in the Information Department. Finally, we should like to acknowledge the patience and skill of Mr Douglas Birch of the Faculty of Arts Photographic Department of Liverpool University.

Keswick   T.K.
1 January 1976   E.K.

I. BOOK PRODUCTION BEFORE PRINTING
A Carmelite friar in his cell, writing. In his left hand he holds a knife, for erasures and for sharpening his quill pen. Nearly a dozen volumes can be glimpsed on the shelves behind him. *British Library*

The Precursors 1

Few public institutions in modern Britain are better known or more popular than our public libraries. Until the local government reforms of 1974–75, there were over 400 library authorities with a total of more than 10,000 branches and other service points, providing for readers throughout the length and breadth of the country – in the big cities, in lonely farmsteads, in remote islands, in hospitals, in old people's homes, even in prisons. At any one time something like one-third of the population, on average, was in library membership.

These were the local libraries, maintained by county, borough, and urban district authorities, and supported from the local rates. In addition there were the great national collections, such as the British Museum Library and the National Libraries of Wales and Scotland. The local libraries are generally reckoned to date from 1850, when the first Public Libraries Act gave local authorities permission to levy a $\frac{1}{2}$d rate for library purposes. The story of the national libraries, which are supported from central government funds, goes back to the foundation of the British Museum in 1753. Long before this, however, there were many libraries which, though they were not as a rule publicly financed, were none the less available for public use. These libraries, which for our present purpose we may call the precursors of the public libraries, form the subject of this chapter.

Mediaeval Origins

For the earliest examples we must go back to the Middle Ages, when books had to be written by hand and were consequently a rare and precious commodity. A single bound volume, in those days, would often cost twenty shillings, which was the equivalent of more than £200 today. Chaucer's clerk of Oxford, who preferred 'Twenty bokes clad in blak or reed, Of Aristotle and his philosophye,' to rich robes and musical instruments, was not perhaps as unworldly as has some-

2. A MONASTIC BOOK CHEST
When books were few they were stored in a book chest, as shown in this picture of Abbot Simon, a twelfth-century abbot of St Albans. *British Library*

3. A MONASTIC BOOK CUPBOARD
At a later stage a book cupboard or even a special bookroom would be needed. Dryburgh Abbey had a bookroom adjoining the parlour, and also a book cupboard, here illustrated, in the cloisters. It would of course be fitted with wooden doors and shelves. *Edith Kelly*

times been made out. Even the largest mediaeval libraries, those of the great Benedictine monasteries of Bury St Edmunds, St Augustine's Abbey at Canterbury, and the Cathedral Priory of Christ Church, Canterbury, numbered only about 2000 volumes each at the end of the fifteenth century, though it is fair to say that a single volume often contained three or four distinct works. The other libraries of this period – in monasteries and friaries, cathedrals and collegiate churches, and universities – seldom possessed more than a few hundred volumes.

In such circumstances the lending of a book was a serious business, and was normally the subject of a formal legal agreement, often involving the deposit by the borrower of a pledge of equal value. Commonly the books were kept under lock and key, or in the case of

4. A MEDIAEVAL
LIBRARY LECTERN
A sophisticated
example from the
library of Lincoln
Cathedral. The books
were chained to the
rod which may be
seen running across
the top of the lectern.
Macmillan

the larger collections chained to lecterns in a special library room. It does seem, however, that the libraries of the monasteries and cathedrals were usually made available for reference purposes to any who might wish to use them. Some time during the latter part of the thirteenth century the Franciscans actually compiled, presumably for the use of their travelling preachers, what we would call a 'union catalogue', listing the works of more than eighty authors in 183 monastic libraries. This manuscript catalogue still survives in the Bodleian Library: it is known as the Register of English Books (*Registrum Librorum Anglie*).

An important limiting factor in the use of these libraries was, of course, the fact that nearly all the books were in Latin. The same was true of the libraries of the non-monastic cathedrals, which were by the close of the Middle Ages virtually chained reference libraries open

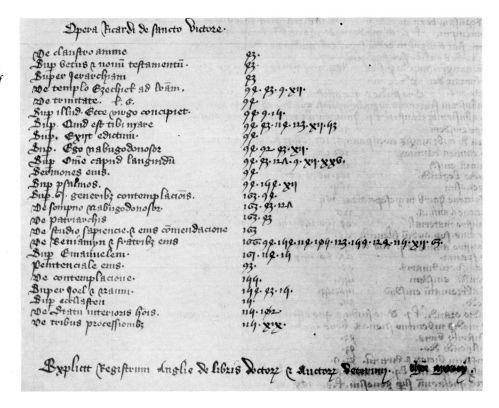

not only to the cathedral and diocesan clergy but also to visiting scholars and students of all kinds. Until the fifteenth century these would almost invariably be clergy, but it should be remembered that at this period the ranks of the clergy included many – clerks, secretaries, stewards, lawyers, teachers, physicians, civil servants – who would now be laymen. Within their limits these libraries were indeed serving the needs of the whole learned order of mediaeval society. The point is illustrated by the inscription in a Latin dictionary presented to York Minster in the late thirteenth century. This is described as

> for the convenience and the use of the priests and clerks frequenting the choir of the aforesaid church, and likewise of other clerks, as well scholars as those at leisure, or travelling, to be placed in a common, safe and honourable place, so that should anyone seek information concerning some point of doubt, scholarship, or disputation, it may easily be found according to the letters of the alphabet.

At a humbler level small collections of books were sometimes kept – locked or chained – in parish churches. A striking example from the later Middle Ages is the collection bequeathed by will of 1492 to the chapel (now parish church) of Pott Shrigley in Cheshire.

6. A MEDIAEVAL BOOKSHOP
It is a mistake to suppose that all mediaeval books were written in monasteries. Many were produced by teams of scribes in commercial *scriptoria*. A fourteenth-century English MS. of a poem called *The Pilgrim* includes this remarkable picture of a traveller visiting a bookshop. *British Library*

7. INSCRIPTION IN A DICTIONARY
Concluding inscription in a Latin dictionary placed in York Minster in the thirteenth century for the use of the cathedral clergy and visiting scholars (see page 12). The second column invokes the customary anathema on anyone removing the book. *York Minster Library*

It included not only a number of service books but also a handful of books of divinity, some of them, apparently, in English, and some of them printed. An early English version of the gospels of St Matthew and St Mark, now in the British Museum Library, was also intended for this library. The books were bequeathed by Geoffrey Downes to the chapel trustees, headed by his cousin Robert Downes, and his will directed that

> if the said Robert or his heirs desire to borrowe any Booke that is Longing to the Chappel, either for himself or any other Gentleman, either for to read or to take a Coppy thereof, that he have such Book as he desireth for the space of 13 weeks; Soe that hee Leave sufficient pledge to keep them safe, and bring them again att the day assigned.

It is reasonable to suppose that the books here referred to were Geoffrey Downes's private library, and the bequest illustrates one of

8. ST CHRISTOPHER'S, POTT SHRIGLEY
The parish church as it is today.

the most significant features of the later Middle Ages, namely the spread of literacy among lay people. This was a reflection of the growing wealth of the country, and a response to the growing needs of government, industry and commerce. Grammar schools became more numerous, elementary schools multiplied, and English came into increasing use as a written language. Chaucer's *Canterbury Tales*, written in the late fourteenth century, are the most illustrious instance of a new body of literature in English, which included not only devotional works but also secular writings such as chronicles, romances and translations from the classics.

Estimates of literacy in early times are notoriously difficult and unreliable, but it is possible to say that by the mid-fifteenth century literacy, in the sense of an ability to read and write in English, was almost universal among the gentry and the merchant class of London and south-east England, and was becoming increasingly common among the ranks of craftsmen and shopkeepers. Many of these people, too, had some competence in Latin. The same statement might hold good of important urban centres outside London, such as Norwich and Bristol, but in Wales and in the rural areas of northern England and Scotland illiteracy must still have been the general rule. Every-

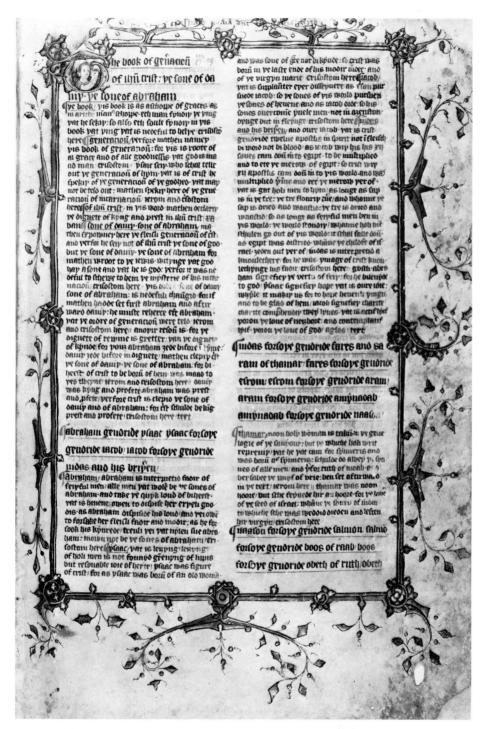

9. MANUSCRIPT INTENDED FOR POTT SHRIGLEY
All the books intended by Geoffrey Downes for the chapel at Pott Shrigley have disappeared except this one, which eventually found its way to the British Museum Library. It is a manuscript dating from about 1400, an early translation of the Gospel of St Matthew and St Mark, with commentary thought to have been composed by John Purvey, secretary and leading disciple of John Wycliffe. The illustration shows the first page of the Gospel of St Matthew. *British Library*

Secchias Was the first Philosophir by Whoom
through the Wil and pleaser of oure lorde god,
Sapience Was vnderstande and laWes receyued . Whiche Sechias saide that euery creature of good, beleue ought to haue in hym sixtene vertues
The first vertue is to drede and, knoWe god, and, his
angellys The seconde vertue is to haue discrecion to discrene the goode from the badde and, to vse vertu and, fle
vices The thride vertue is to obeye the kynges or princes
that god hath ordeygned to regyne vpon hym and that
haue lordship and, poWer vpon the people The fourthe.
vertue is to Worship hys fadre & hys modre The fyfthe
vertue is to do Justely and, truely to euery creature aftir
his possibilite The sixthe vertue is to distribute his almes to the puer people. The seuenthe vertue is to kepe
and, defende straungers and, pilgrymes The eyghte
vertue is to kynde and, determine him self to serue our lorde
god, The nynthe vertue is to escheWe fornicacion The
tenthe vertue is to haue pacience. The enleuenth vertue
is to be stedfast and, true The tWelfthe vertue is to
be peasible and, attemperate and, shamfast of synne The
therteenthe vertue is to loue Justice The fourtenthe vertue is to be liberal and, not couetoup The fyftenthe vertue is to offre sacrifices to our lord god, almyghty for the
benefices and, graces that he sheWeth hym dayly The
sixtenthe vertue is to Worship god, almyghty and, to put
hym hoolp in his protection and, defence for resistence of the
in fortunitees that dayly falles in thys Worlde The saide
Sechias saide that right as it apparteineth to the people

II. AN EARLY PRINTING PRESS
From the title page of Plato's Works, printed at
Florence by Jodocus Badius Ascenius in 1518.
Norfolk County Library

10. ENGLAND'S
FIRST PRINTED
BOOK
The first page of
Caxton's *Dictes or
Sayengis of the
Philosophres*, 1477.

where the standard of literacy amongst men was higher than amongst
women.

So long as books had to be produced by hand, of course, reading
for other than business purposes was bound to be limited. It was the
advent of printing which really revolutionised the situation, and
made possible, ultimately, the development of both private and public
libraries on a large scale. As is well known, it was William Caxton who
introduced the art to this country, and who in 1477 produced, on his
press at Westminster, England's first printed book, the *Dictes or
Sayengis of the Philosophres*.

Britain's first public libraries, however, belong to the manuscript
age. There are three of which record has so far come to light. The
first, not surprisingly, was in London, and was associated with the
name of that famous London citizen, Richard Whittington. Dying
childless in 1423, Whittington left all his great fortune to charity,
and two years later his executors joined forces with those of another
wealthy London mercer, William Bury, to establish and present to
the City of London a library for public use. This library, handsomely

This deathbed scene is reproduced from the original ordin-
ances of the hospital or almshouse of St Michael Royal in the
City of London, which, like the
Guildhall Library, was established by Whittington's executors. The chief executor, John
Carpenter, is seen in the left
foreground. Also included in the
picture are two other executors,
a priest, a doctor, and at the foot
of the bed (in anticipation) the
thirteen poor men for whom the
almshouse was intended, headed
by their tutor. *Mercers' Company*

accommodated in a new building adjoining the Guildhall, seems to
have been, after the manner of the time, a chained library, and mainly
theological in character, the public for whom it was intended being
clergy and students. This is illustrated by the will of Whittington's
chief executor, John Carpenter, who in 1442 bequeathed books to
the library 'for the profit of the students there, and those discoursing
to the common people'.

The first Guildhall library (the present Guildhall library dates
from the nineteenth century) was in its earlier years well used, one of
the chaplains of the Guildhall College normally acting as librarian.
It survived until 1549, when the books were carried off by agents of the

13. ALL SAINTS' CHURCH, BRISTOL
In this old engraving of the church, from William Barrett's *History and Antiquities of the City of Bristol*, 1789, the library room of the Gild of Kalendars may be seen behind the parapet over the north aisle between the tower on the left and the priest's house on the right. It survived until 1782. *Avon County Library*

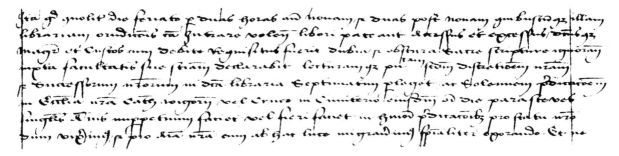

14. INSTRUCTIONS FOR A LIBRARIAN
These few lines in a Bishop's Register incorporate instructions to the keepers of the fifteenth-century public libraries at Worcester and Bristol (see below).
Hereford and Worcester Record Office

Lord Protector, the Duke of Somerset, 'with promise to be restored shortly'. They were, in fact, never returned.

A namesake or perhaps a relative of Whittington's chief executor was John Carpenter, Bishop of Worcester, who a little later in the century established rather similar libraries at Worcester and Bristol. That at Worcester, founded about 1458, must have been intended not for the monks of the cathedral priory, who had their own monastic library, but for the secular clergy. It was attached, rather grimly, to the chantry of the cathedral charnel-house, with the chaplain as librarian. In Bristol, which was not then a cathedral city, the library was founded in 1464, and was attached to the Gild of Kalendars – a religious guild associated with the church of All Saints – with the prior of the Gild as librarian. Regulations drawn up for both libraries prescribed that the books should be chained and catalogued; that the librarian should be a bachelor of divinity, or at least a graduate, sufficiently instructed in Holy Scripture, and a ready preacher; and that

> on every weekday, for two hours before None and two hours after None, all who wish to enter that library for the purpose of study shall be free to come and go; and the aforesaid Master and Keeper shall, when duly required, expound doubtful and obscure passages of Holy Scripture to the ignorant, to the best of his knowledge.

It should perhaps be explained that the time at which the office of None was celebrated varied from 2 p.m. to 4 p.m. according to the season of the year.

The later history of these two libraries is obscure, but there is some evidence to suggest that they may have survived into the sixteenth century. Like the Guildhall library, however, they must have disappeared at the time of the Reformation.

Renaissance and Reformation

When we look back on these early libraries, it is clear that they are part of the fabric of the mediaeval church. Even when they are open to all comers, and may reasonably be described as public, their purpose is still basically religious, their clientèle basically clerical. At the time of the Reformation, in the middle years of the sixteenth century, the monastic libraries and most of the cathedral and church libraries were either destroyed or dispersed, many of the books being condemned as heretical and superstitious. Later, when the worst of the destruction was over, the scattered remnants were gathered by private collectors and many ultimately found their way into the British Museum Library or some other great public repository. In the meantime, the task of creating libraries to meet the needs of a new age had to be started almost from the beginning.

The complex of ideas and events which we refer to as the Renaissance and the Reformation finally ended the clerical monopoly of learning, and led to a society in which the lay and ecclesiastical elements were more evenly balanced. The change is plain if we compare the gift of the Guildhall library made by Whittington's executors with the creation of Gresham College by the executors of Sir Thomas Gresham. Like Whittington, Gresham was a wealthy London mercer, but the money he bequeathed to the City and the Mercers' Company in 1579 was used not to found an ecclesiastical establishment but to establish a college 'for the common benefit of the people of this city . . . for such citizens and others, as have small knowledge of the Latin tongue'. Courses were to be given in divinity ('that the common people be well grounded in the chief points of the Christian religion'), civil law, physic, rhetoric, geometry (including arithmetic), astronomy (including geography and navigation) and music (including practical exercises 'by concert of voice or of instruments').

The level of literacy continued to rise. Grammar schools, offering a classical education, numbered between three and four hundred by the end of the sixteenth century, and half as many again by 1650; and there were numerous more elementary schools – town or village schools, often private venture schools – where for a modest charge children could acquire the rudiments of letters. A good deal of illiteracy persisted, of course, among the lower orders and in the rural areas, but on the whole the extent of literacy was greater than is often supposed. Already in the Elizabethan age it seems that the ability to read, write and keep accounts was widespread down to the level of the tradesman and the craftsman in the towns and the yeoman farmer in the country, even if these skills were rarely used. In the seventeenth century we must suppose that increasing facilities for education brought a further improvement. When George Fox, the Quaker, addressing a field meeting in Leominster in 1657, was challenged on a point of doctrine, he was able to call on those present to take out their Bibles and look up the relevant passage.

This incident illustrates another factor in the situation, namely the increased availability of books. By the mid-sixteenth century printing was firmly established as the normal method of book production. Religious texts still dominated the scene, and long continued to form the largest single category of published works, but secular literature in English was steadily increasing in range and variety, and the Elizabethan reader could take his choice among chronicles and histories, travel books, romances, jest books, ballads, herbals, books on etiquette, and popular guides to medicine, natural history and astronomy. In the seventeenth century, with such writers as Shakespeare and Milton, Bacon and Newton, Hobbes and Locke, Clarendon and Fuller, English literature really came into its own.

We must not, however, paint too favourable a picture. Though many people could read, it seems clear that only a small minority of people, chiefly in London and the university towns, were really conversant with books and in the habit of regular reading; and that a still smaller number had anything that could be called a library. Apart from the occasional cultivated merchant or country gentleman, the regular use of books was still in the main something for the learned professions – university scholars, lawyers, physicians, clergymen, and the growing army of schoolmasters.

Early Town and Parish Libraries

The needs of these groups in the community, and especially of the clergy, were met in the post-Reformation period mainly by what may most conveniently be called endowed libraries – using that term to cover libraries created by gift even though in most cases no provision was made for a continuing income. Most of these libraries were the gift of a single benefactor. A clergyman would bequeath his personal library for the use of his successors; a bishop would endow a library in the church of his native parish; a country gentleman or a wealthy burgess would found a library as an act of piety or civic pride. Usually the library was placed under the control of the parochial authorities, and housed in or near the church, but this was not invariable: in corporate towns the library was often under the control of the municipal authorities, or of the town and a parish jointly; some libraries were placed in grammar schools, a few in the hands of trustees. Whatever the form of government, these libraries had certain features in common. They were usually small – rarely more than 1000 volumes; and at the outset they were intended primarily for the use of the clergy, and consisted mainly of theological literature, much of it in Latin. Often, like mediaeval libraries, they were chained, a practice that continued, in many instances, into the eighteenth century.

The attention paid to the needs of the clergy derives from the emphasis placed by the Protestant religion upon the reading and exposition of the Bible. Protestantism is, as has often been pointed out, a book religion, and it was deemed of great importance that the clergy should be provided with the books they needed for the study of the sacred text. In many places, indeed, the Puritans created special preaching lectureships to supplement the services of the parish clergy. At the same time indications of non-clerical use are not entirely lacking, especially as we move into the seventeenth century.

A few examples of libraries founded during the first hundred years or so after the Reformation will illustrate the variety of the arrangements made. At this period provision was most commonly made in the cities and market towns. Some of the earliest examples were in Scotland, the most notable being at Dundee, where a library attached to St Mary's Church came into existence some time before the close of the sixteenth century. It was founded, apparently, by William Christison, minister there from 1560 to 1598, and was initially under the joint control of the minister and the town council. Augmented by many gifts, it continued in active service throughout the seventeenth and early eighteenth centuries.

The town library at Leicester was originally established at St Martin's Church, in or before 1587, reputedly by Henry, Third Earl of Huntingdon, a zealous Puritan who maintained a preacher in the church at his own expense. The library was later taken over by the Corporation and transferred to the Guildhall. At Grantham, in Lincolnshire, in 1598, Francis Trigge, a local clergyman, gave books to the value of about £100 to the alderman and burgesses and the clergy of St Wulfram's. They were to be chained in a room over the south porch 'for the better encreasinge of learninge . . . by such of the cleargie and others as well beinge inhabitantes in or near Grantham and the soake thereof as in other places in the said Countie'. At Ipswich in Suffolk a year later, Alderman William Smart, draper, bequeathed about thirty Latin books and manuscripts to the church of St Mary Tower, for the use of 'the common preacher of the Town for the time being, or any other preacher minded to preach in the said parish church'. At Norwich, in 1608, the city authorities converted three rooms in the house of Jerrom Goodwyn, swordbearer, into 'a lybrary for the use of preachers, and for a lodging chamber for such preachers as shall come to this cittie'. And at Bristol in 1615

15. THE OLD TOWN
LIBRARY AT
LEICESTER
This picture of the old
town library in the
Guildhall is from a
painting by Alice M.
Hobson, dated 1900.
*Leicestershire
Museums*

Redwood, gentleman, gave a house to the city 'to be con-
to a Librayre, or place to put bookes for the furtherance of
inge'. As usual, this was a theological library, most of the 186
d volumes recorded in 1640 being in Latin or Greek.

Bury in Lancashire, some time before 1634, Henry Bury, clerk,
over 600 books to trustees 'for the use of Bury parish and the
trie therabouts of ministers also at ther metinge and of schole
isters and others that seek for learninge and knowledge'. Bury was
a corporate town, and this library seems shortly to have passed
the local grammar school. It does not follow, however, that it
hereby ceased to fulfil any public function, for we have several
examples of school libraries serving a wider purpose. This was the
case at Shrewsbury School, where the library founded in 1596
developed in the following century into a public library, and eventually
in the eighteenth century into a lending library for the whole county.
At Lewisham, in 1652, on the initiative of the vicar, Abraham Colfe, a
library was established in the grammar school for the use of local

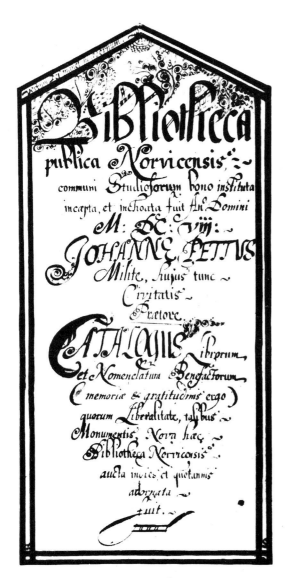

16. THE OLD TOWN LIBRARY AT NORWICH
Left Title-page of the Donation Book, written on vellum, begun in 1659. Note the very early use of the term 'public library' (*bibliotheca publica*). *Right* First printed catalogue, 1706. Even from this one page the ecclesiastical flavour of the collection is clear. The second book listed, *Antichristi demonstratio* by Robert Abbot, Bishop of Salisbury, dates from the library's first year, 1608. *Norfolk County Library*

ministers and gentry. It is probably true to say that in those days any library attached to a public institution tended to be made available, as far as practicable, to the entire learned community.

Quite the most remarkable of the early town libraries was Chetham's Library, Manchester, founded by Humphrey Chetham, a wealthy woollen and linen merchant, and according to Fuller 'a diligent

*Received of the Mayor and Burgesses
of Kings Lyn Two Pounds for one years
Salary due at Michaelmas 1778.
C. Phelpes, Librarian.*

17. RECEIPT FOR A LIBRARIAN'S SALARY
The library founded at St Margaret's, King's Lynn, was a church library under municipal control, and was at first a lending library, but lending was forbidden in 1657 owing to the number of books lost. The £2 salary suggests that the post of librarian was part-time. *Norfolk County Library*

reader of the Scriptures, and of the works of sound divines'. At his death in 1653 Chetham bequeathed £1000 and the residue of his estate for the establishment of a chained library 'for the use of schollars and others well affected to resort unto . . . the same bookes there to remain as a publick library forever'. Since Manchester, like Bury, was still unincorporated, the library was placed in the hands of trustees, who very wisely invested the residue of the estate in land to provide an income for the purchase of books. It was this permanent endowment which enabled Chetham's Library (unlike so many other early libraries) to grow steadily over the years and adapt itself to changing needs. Though it was at the outset dominantly theological, the trustees evidently took a liberal view of the professional and leisure-time needs of all the educated people of the town, and by 1684 the collection of nearly 3000 volumes included fairly substantial sections on history, travel, topography, law, medicine and science. The chaining of books was abandoned about 1745, but the library continued to be for reference only, with locked gates guarding each alcove.

Of the numerous libraries under parochial control the most striking was that of St Mary's, Langley Marish, Buckinghamshire, founded in 1623 by a local landowner, Sir John Kederminster, 'as well for the perpetual benefit of the vicar and curate of the parish of Langley, as for all other ministers and preachers of God's word that would resort thither'. This library is of special interest partly because it was housed in a beautiful panelled room constructed for the purpose in the old church porch; and partly because of the unusual arrange-

18. THE OLD GRAMMAR SCHOOL LIBRARY, GUILDFORD
Originally a town library, and known to have been in existence as early as 1573, this library was appropriated to the school by the end of the century, but probably continued to meet public needs. The chained books on the right show the customary way of shelving such books, i.e. with the fore-edge outward. This was because the chain was normally attached to the front edge of the cover. *Royal Grammar School, Guildford*

ments made for the safe keeping of the books. They were not chained, but the key of the library room was placed in the custody of four poor people dwelling in the almshouse that Kederminster had also founded, and it was provided that when any person desired to use the library one of these four at least should

attend within the door of the said library, and not depart from thence during all the time that any person should remain therein, and should all that while keep the key of the said door fastened with a chain unto one of their girdles and should also take special care that no books be lent or purloined out of the said library,

19. LEWISHAM GRAMMAR SCHOOL
A public library was established here, on the initiative of the vicar, in 1652. This picture of the school is reproduced from the catalogue of the library published in 1831.

but that every book should be duly placed in their room, and that the room should be kept clean.

Alongside these libraries for the learned orders of society a small but increasing provision was beginning to be made for the less learned. As early as 1536 Thomas Cromwell, Vicar-General to Henry VIII, had prescribed that every parish must provide a copy of the complete Bible, in English as well as in Latin, 'and lay the same in the choir, for every man that will to look and read thereon'. In later injunctions, only the English Bible was insisted upon, but other works were added, such as Bishop John Jewel's *Apology in Defence of the Church of England*, and John Foxe's *Book of Martyrs*. By the middle of the seventeenth century most parish churches had a few books of this kind, commonly chained to a lectern or a reading desk. Sometimes secular works were included: for example the parish church of Easton-in-Gordano, near Bristol, had a folio volume on mathematics, *The Mariner's or Artizan's Magazine*, presented by the author Captain Samuel Sturmy, for the use of this and neighbouring parishes.

Though chained, it might be borrowed on a security of £3.

At the parish church of Repton in Derbyshire, in 1622, William Bladon gave a small collection of unchained books – a Bible, 'two bookes of Martters', Perkins on the Creed, Dod and Cleaver on the Commandments, and other English devotional works, to be lent at the discretion of the vicar and churchwardens 'to anie of the parrishe of Reptoun for the space of one 2 or 3 moneths', provided only that any damage to the books should be made good by the borrower. This liberal provision for lending is very remarkable at this early date, and indeed if fifteen volumes can be regarded as a library, this is the earliest recorded free public lending library in Britain.

Humphrey Chetham of Manchester, besides providing in his will for the scholars' library already described, bequeathed funds for the establishment of no fewer than five parish libraries in and around Manchester, to contain such 'godly English Bookes' as his executors should think 'most proper for the edificacion of the common people, to be chained uppon deskes, or to bee fixed to the pillars or in other convenient places'. In assessing the impact of provision of this kind the passionate interest in devotional reading which was characteristic of the sixteenth and seventeenth centuries should not be underestimated. To us the surviving volumes seem dauntingly theological, but it would be wrong to suppose they were not read by some at least of the parishioners. At Wootton Wawen in Warwickshire 'some good books' bequeathed in 1652 by the vicar, George Dunscomb, for the use of his parishioners, were at first kept in the vicarage, but in 1693 the parishioners insisted that they must be brought out and chained to a desk in the church.

21. THE PARISH LIBRARY AT LANGLEY MARISH
Founded by Sir John Kederminster in 1623, this library is beautifully housed in
the church porch. Sir John's portrait may be dimly seen inside the cupboard door,
top left. Expertly restored during the present century, both books and furnishings
may now be seen almost in their pristine condition. The books are mainly late
16th and early 17th century divinity. *Country Life*

Opposite:
22. TITLE-PAGE OF THE GREAT ENGLISH BIBLE OF 1539
This English translation of the Bible, prepared by Miles Coverdale and incorporating some of the work of the martyred William Tyndale, was from the time of its
publication the officially authorised version, chained for public use in churches
throughout the country. Henry VIII is seated in majesty at the head of the page,
while at the foot the populace shouts 'Vivat Rex!' 'God Save the Kinge!'

23. CHAINED COPY OF BISHOP JEWEL'S 'DEFENSE OF THE APOLOGIE OF THE CHURCHE OF ENGLANDE'
This was one of Jewel's later works, published in 1571. For nearly four hundred years it reposed on its lectern in the parish church of Great Durnford, Wiltshire, but in 1970 it was stolen, and it has not been recovered.
Council for Places of Worship

24. BOLTON SCHOOL LIBRARY
This library, pictured as it was in the late nineteenth century, incorporated the remains of the chained library bequeathed by Humphrey Chetham to Bolton Parish Church in 1553.

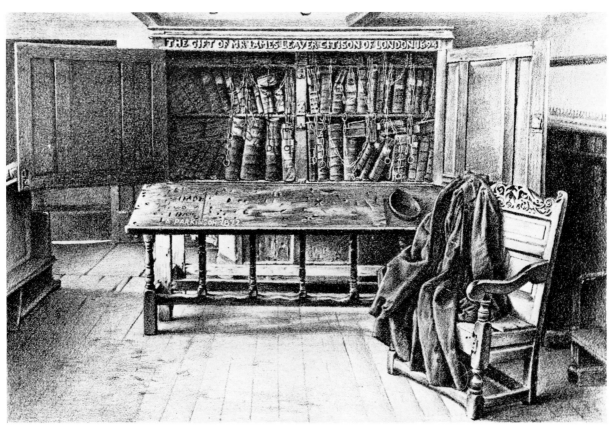

Later Town and Parish Libraries

The movement for the founding of town and parish libraries was at its height around the year 1700: of the two hundred or so libraries established between 1550 and 1800 about eighty came into existence in the forty years between 1680 and 1720. Libraries continued to be founded here and there well into the nineteenth century, but comparatively few can be assigned to the period after 1770.

The sudden burst of activity at the close of the seventeenth century can be linked with the new spirit of piety – a reaction, perhaps, against the laxity of the Restoration period – which manifested itself at this time in the formation of religious societies, and led on in the eighteenth century to Methodism and Evangelicalism. It can also be linked, quite unmistakeably, with the movement for popular religious education which found its expression in the thousands of charity schools established during the eighteenth century for the education of the children of the poor – a movement in which the lead was taken by the Society for Promoting Christian Knowledge, founded in 1699, and its sister organisation the Society in Scotland for Propagating Christian Knowledge.

Because so many of the cities and market towns were already in some degree provided for, most of the post-1680 foundations were parochial libraries in the smaller centres of population, especially in rural areas such as East Anglia and the North of England. In general these libraries followed the seventeenth-century pattern, but as time went on some at least began to develop in the direction of the modern public library. Instead of being founded exclusively for the use of the clergy, they were made available, as at Rotherham in 1704, for 'clergy and parishioners', or as at Nottingham in 1744, 'for the use of the Clergy, Lawyers, Phicitians, and other persons of a liberal and learned education', or even more widely, as at Lewes in 1717, 'for the benefit of the inhabitants'. In some instances, the books became available on a subscription basis. The content of these libraries, too, tended to become less exclusively ecclesiastical: theological and devotional literature was still there in plenty, but there was also a wide range of more general literature, and there were more books in English. From the early eighteenth century, moreover, the chaining of books became less common (the parish library at All Saints', Hereford, in 1715, was the last to be established as a chained library); and this facilitated the development of lending facilities in a number of places. Loans were, however, still normally hedged round with a variety of cautions and restrictions, and payment of a deposit was often called for. Rev. Robert Thomlinson, who in 1735–45 presented some 4600 volumes to the ancient parochial library of St Nicholas,

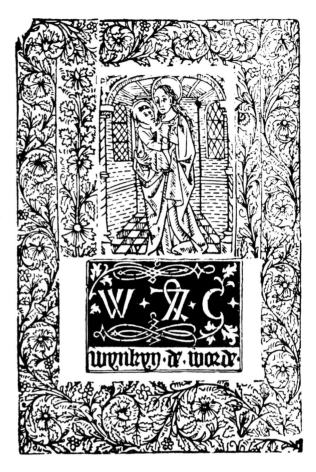

25. ALL SAINTS' PARISH LIBRARY, HEREFORD
One of two bookcases housing the library of about 300 volumes of 'Divinity, Morality and History', bequeathed by Dr William Brewster, physician, in 1715 – the last example of the establishment of a chained library. In 1858 a bookseller-churchwarden arranged for it to be sold off to America, but it was rescued in the nick of time. *F. C. Morgan*

26. A PARISH LIBRARY TREASURE
The old endowed libraries often included works of great bibliographical rarity. The book of which the final page is here illustrated is one of our very earliest printed works, an *Exposition of the Sarum Hymns and Sequences* printed by Wynkyn de Worde in 1502. It is in the Nantwich Parish Church Library, founded about 1700. *St Mary's Church, Nantwich*

Newcastle upon Tyne, made the curious regulation that none of his books should be lent except to 'one that is going to publish a Book of at least 300 Pages in Octavo', and even then only on deposit of twice the value of the book concerned, to be forfeited if it was not returned on time.

In selecting a few only of the parish libraries of this period for mention here, we may well begin with Archbishop Tenison's Library at St Martin's in the Fields, London. Founded in 1684 by the vicar, Thomas Tenison, who afterwards became Archbishop of

Canterbury, it was housed in a special building designed by Christopher Wren and erected in St Martin's churchyard. It was a substantial collection of books (about 7000 titles in a catalogue of 1707–9), intended 'for public use' but especially for the use of the vicar and lecturer of St Martin's, the schoolmaster and usher, the clergy of neighbouring churches, and the King's chaplains in ordinary. This was the only library of its kind in London at this time, though Sion College – a college and almshouse for clergy – had a library established in 1630 which to some extent met the needs of the clergy in the City. In the meantime there were many complaints about the lack of library facilities in the capital. John Evelyn, who assisted Wren in preparing the plans for Tenison's Library, thought it 'a great reproach . . . that so great a city as London should not have a public library becoming it'.

Oddly enough Kirkwall, capital of far-away Orkney, had a parish library before London, for in 1683 William Baikie, a Stronsay land-

27. ARCHBISHOP TENISON'S LIBRARY, ST MARTIN'S IN THE FIELDS
Notice once more the association of a library with a school, in this case a grammar school. *Westminster City Libraries*

28. SCHOOL AND LIBRARY AT KING'S CLIFFE, NORTHAMPTONSHIRE
Above The elementary school founded at King's Cliffe in 1752 by a native of that place, William Law, author of the *Serious Call* and other devotional works. The schoolmaster's house is on the left. *Malcolm Seaborne*
Right Close-up of the door of the schoolmaster's house, bearing the inscription, 'Books of Piety are here lent to any Persons of this or ye Neighbouring Towns.' *Malcolm Seaborne*

owner, bequeathed eight score volumes to the minister of Kirkwall and his successors, 'to be keepte and used be him for a publick liberarie as said is, within the Town of Kirkwall'. This library, mainly at the outset of religious books, was evidently highly prized, for it was maintained and enlarged by local contributions. Some 600 volumes still survive in the library of Aberdeen University.

The parish library at Wimborne Minster in Dorset, which originated with a bequest by the vicar, William Stone, in 1685, and was later added to, was a chained library in the old tradition. Its 240 surviving volumes are very typical, including a few classics, five Bibles, some general and ecclesiastical history, the works of the Fathers, and much post-Reformation theology and devotional literature. A considerable number of the books are in Latin. By contrast the library bequeathed to the parish of Henley on Thames in 1737 by its rector, Dr Charles Aldrich, included a high proportion of English works, and reflected the interests of a cultivated country

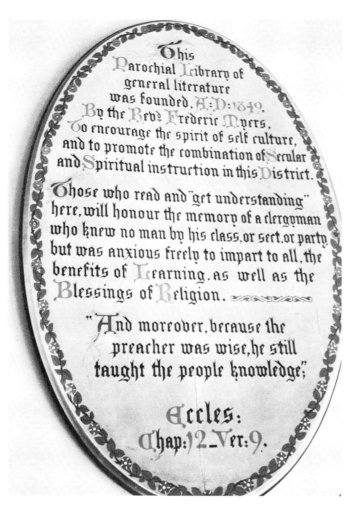

29. INSCRIPTION IN ST JOHN'S LIBRARY, KESWICK
Comparatively few endowed parish libraries can be assigned to the period after 1770. The library at St John's, Keswick, founded by the vicar in 1849 to meet the needs of a new parish, is an exception. It had a long and successful life until eventually taken over by Cumberland County Library in 1958.
Edith Kelly

gentleman. Three of the fourteen sections into which the catalogue was divided were indeed taken up with religious literature; the classics occupied a fourth, general and ecclesiastical history a fifth, and philosophy, education and morals a sixth. But the remaining sections included such diverse subjects as languages; geography and travel; poetry and fine arts; architecture and music; agriculture and natural history; and medicine and anatomy. Such a library obviously had the makings of a genuine public library, and when it came into use it was in fact thrown open for reading and borrowing by all parishioners liable to church rates. To begin with, however, it was impounded by Aldrich's successor, and forty years went by before the parish secured possession of it.

Among non-parochial libraries the two most unusual were those at Innerpeffray and at Bamburgh Castle. The library at Innerpeffray stands in a remote spot beside the River Earn, in Perthshire. It was founded by David Drummond, third Lord Madertie, about 1694,

30. INNERPEFFRAY
LIBRARY
A view of the library
(*left*) and chapel from
the River Earn.
Innerpeffray Trustees

and was originally housed in the family chapel, but a separate building was erected in the middle of the following century. By 1747 at the latest it was a lending library. It had originally been founded and endowed 'for the benefit and encouragement of young students', but it also attracted ministers, schoolmasters, and people of many other trades and professions. The barber, the weaver, the farmer, the miller, the tailor, the merchant, the surgeon are among those who appear in the eighteenth-century list of borrowers. Many came from considerable distances, often fording the river to reach their goal. The success of this institution (still existing today with more than 3000 volumes) is a remarkable tribute to the Scottish zeal for education at this period. Not surprisingly, religious works figured largely both in the collection and in the list of borrowings, but history also occupied a significant place, and the most borrowed work was the *History of Charles V*, by William Robertson, principal of Edinburgh University, which was published in 1769 and was something of a bestseller at that time.

The Bamburgh story is a curious one. Nathaniel Crew, who was appointed Bishop of Durham in 1674 and in later life became also the third and last Baron Crew, died in 1721 leaving large benefactions to charity. At Bamburgh Castle his bequest was used to establish a whole range of welfare services for the people of the neighbourhood, including schools and a dispensary for the poor. It was in this setting that there was created, in 1778, a public library which by the mid-nineteenth century had attained the then substantial proportions of 6000 volumes. According to rules drawn up in 1810 the library was open for reference on Saturdays from 10 a.m. to 1 p.m., and books might be borrowed by any well known housekeeper living within twenty miles of the castle, and any clergyman of any denomination holding a benefice within the same area.

The second half of the eighteenth century brought the foundation of two notable town libraries. At Preston in 1761 Dr William Shepherd, a local medical man who had twice served as mayor of the town, bequeathed his books and a small endowment to provide a reference library for the use of the mayor and corporation and such other persons as they or any of them might permit. The interest on a sum of £200 was to provide an honorarium for the librarian, and the interest on a further £1000 was to provide for the maintenance and enlargement of the library. Though the endowment was not large, the civic authorities were conscientious in providing a home for the library, and in making it available for public use. From 1836 it was open not only in the daytime, from 10 to 4 daily, but also – and this was quite exceptional at this period – in the evenings from 6 to 9.45. Applicants had to be approved by one of the trustees, and since

31. BAMBURGH CASTLE
A view of the Castle from the sea, from an engraving of 1813.

32. THE BRAY LIBRARIES
Top left The founder, Dr Thomas Bray, from a painting by an unknown artist.
United Society for the Propagation of the Gospel
Top right Bray Library bookplate, from the library founded at Darowen in
Montgomeryshire in 1710.

they were also required to pay 3s for a copy of the printed catalogue
it may be assumed that they were drawn from the ranks of the more
well-to-do citizenry.

Unlike most of the libraries so far described this was a general not a
theological collection, though it naturally reflected the special
interests of the founder. For this reason it included not only, as we
should expect, many medical books, but also many examples of fine
printing, ranging from very early printed works to John Baskerville's
Virgil of 1757, the first publication of one of England's finest typo-
graphers.

The Shepherd Library was eventually absorbed into the Preston
Public Library, which opened in 1879. A similar development
occurred at Glasgow, where in 1791 Walter Stirling, merchant,
bequeathed to the Lord Provost and his successors the sum of £1000,
together with certain property, in order to ensure 'the constant and
perpetual existence of a Public Library for the Citizens of Glasgow'.
Unfortunately the bequest was not sufficient for the purposes the

Top left Part of the catalogue of the Bray Library established at Corston, Somerset, in 1710. *United Society for the Propagation of the Gospel*
Top right Bray bookcase at Bridlington. Inside the door are pasted, above, a list of the books, and below, a copy of the Parochial Libraries Act of 1709 (illustrated below, p. 43). *Council for Places of Worship*

testator had in mind, and the directors appointed under the terms of the will decided to restrict its use to those paying a substantial life subscription. On this basis, by the middle of the following century, a collection of over 11,000 books was accumulated, and from 1848 these were made accessible to the public for reference purposes. In 1871 the library was united with another subscription library, the so-called 'Glasgow Public Library', but eventually in 1912 arrangements were made for it to be absorbed into the Glasgow City Library, under whose auspices it eventually developed into the main central lending collection.

More Libraries for the Clergy

The eighteenth century brought renewed efforts to make provision for the reading needs of the clergy. In England the initiative in this matter was taken by an Anglican parson, Dr Thomas Bray, who was also one of the leading founders, in 1699, of the Society for Promoting

Christian Knowledge. Two years earlier, in an *Essay towards promoting all Necessary and Useful Knowledge, both Divine and Human, in all parts of his Majesty's Dominions*, he set forth a rather grandiose scheme for a lending library in each deanery for clergy and gentry; smaller libraries for the country clergy; and laymen's libraries for the use of parishioners – all these to be maintained by public subscription. The proposal for laymen's libraries never came to anything, but by Bray's own efforts and those of his friends, and after his death in 1730 by the efforts of a trust known as the Associates of Dr Bray, considerable progress was made in the provision of clerical libraries. At first the emphasis was on small collections of theological works for the use of the country clergy, many of whom, struggling to make ends meet on an income of £30 a year or less, were quite unable to purchase books for themselves. These libraries were for the exclusive use of the incumbent concerned. After 1768, however, the Associates concentrated their main effort on the provision of lending libraries, which were situated for the most part in the market towns and so could serve the needs of a whole district. By 1800 the total number of Bray libraries was nearly 200.

About one-third of these libraries were in Wales, where very few endowed libraries had been established. The Bray libraries were particularly welcome to a poverty-stricken and often ill-educated clergy, and form a parallel to the strenuous efforts being made by the SPCK, and especially by Rev. Griffith Jones, Rector of Llanddowror in Carmarthenshire, to educate the Welsh laity. The 'circulating schools' established by Griffith Jones, which moved round from village to village providing instruction in reading (in Welsh) to all comers young and old, claimed to have enrolled more than 300,000 pupils between 1737 and 1779, and many more were taught in evening classes.

For Scotland an even more grandiose scheme was proposed in 1699 by James Kirkwood, an ejected Episcopalian minister, in an essay entitled *Overture for Founding and Maintaining of Bibliothecks in every Paroch throughout this Kingdom*. Kirkwood wished to see, in each parish, a free public lending library, financed by an annual levy on the minister and landholders, and stocked 'not only with all the valuable and useful Old Books in any Art or Science, but also with all the valuable New Books, as soon as they are even heard of or seen in the World'. The schoolmaster or reader was to act as librarian. Such a scheme was, of course, quite impracticable, but at Kirkwood's insistence the Church Assembly did provide a number of small libraries for the presbyteries and parishes of the Highlands and Islands. Unlike the Bray libraries, these were not restricted to the clergy: the books were available for borrowing by any Protestant, but

Anno Septimo *ANNÆ REGINÆ*.

An Act for the better Preservation of Parochial Libraries in that Part of *Great Britain* called *England*.

Hereas in many Places in the South Parts of *Great Britain* called *England* and *Wales*, the Provision for the Clergy is so Mean, that the necessary Expence of Books for the better Prosecution of their Studies cannot be Defrayed by them ; And whereas of late Years, several Charitable and Well-disposed Persons have by Charitable Contributions, Erected Libraries within several Parishes and Districts in *England* and *Wales* ; But some Provision is wanting to Preserve the same, and such others as shall be Provided in the same manner, from Embezelment : Be it therefore Enacted by the Queens most Excellent Majesty, by and with the Advice and Consent of the Lords Spiritual and Temporal, and Commons in this present Parliament Assembled, and by the Authority of the same, That in every Parish or Place where such a Library is or shall be erected, the same shall be preserved for such Use and Uses, as the same is and shall be given, and the Orders and Rules of the Founder or Founders of such Libraries shall be observed and kept.

And for the Encouragement of such Founders and Benefactors, and to the Intent they may be Satisfied, that their Pious and Charitable Intent may not be Frustrated, Be it also Enacted by the Authority aforesaid, That every Incumbent, Rector, Vicar, Minister, or Curate of a Parish, before he shall be permitted to Use and Enjoy such Library, shall enter into such Security by Bond, or otherwise, for Preservation of such Library, and due Observance of the Rules and Orders belonging to the same, as the proper Ordinaries within their respective Jurisdictions in their Discretion shall think fit; and in case any Book or Books belonging to the said Library shall be taken away and Detained, it shall and may be Lawful for the said Incumbent, Rector, Vicar, Minister, or Curate for the time being, or any other Person or Persons, to bring an Action of Trover and Conversion, in the Name of the proper Ordinaries within their respective Jurisdictions, whereupon Treble Damages shall be given with full Costs of Suit, as if the same were his or their proper Book or Books, which Damages shall be applied to the Use and Benefit of the said Library.

And it is further Enacted by the Authority aforesaid, That it shall and may be Lawful to and for the proper Ordinary, or his Commissary or Official in his respective Jurisdiction, or the Arch-Deacon, or by his Direction his Official or Surrogate, if the said Arch-Deacon be not the Incumbent of the Place where such Library is, in his or their respective Visitation, to enquire into the State and Condition of the said Libraries, and to amend and redress the Grievances and Defects of and concerning the same, as to him or them shall seem meet ; and it shall and may be Lawful to and for the proper Ordinary from time to time, as often as shall be thought fit, to appoint such Person or Persons as he shall think fit, to View the State and Condition of such Libraries, and the said Ordinaries, Arch-Deacons or Officials respectively, shall have free Access to the same at such times as they shall respectively Appoint.

And be it also further Enacted by the Authority aforesaid, That where any Library is Appropriated to the Use of the Minister of any Parish or Place, every Rector, Vicar, Minister or Curate of the same, within Six Months after his Institution, Induction or Admission, shall make or cause to be made a New Catalogue of all Books remaining in, or belonging to such Library, and shall Sign the said Catalogue, thereby acknowledging the Custody and Possession of the said Books ; which said Catalogue so Signed, shall be delivered to the proper Ordinary within the time aforesaid, to be kept or Registred in his Court, without any Fee or Reward for the same.

And be it further Enacted by the Authority aforesaid, That where there are any Parochial Libraries already Erected, the Incumbent, Rector, Vicar, Minister, or Curate of such Parish or Place, shall make or cause to be made a Catalogue of all Books in the same, thereby acknowledging

the Custody and Possession thereof, which Catalogue so Signed, shall be delivered to the proper Ordinary, on or before the Nine and twentieth day of *September*, which shall be in the Year of our Lord One thousand seven hundred and nine ; and where any Library shall at any time hereafter be Given and Appropriated to the Use of any Parish or Place, where there shall be an Incumbent, Rector, Vicar, Minister, or Curate in Possession, such Incumbent, Rector, Vicar, Minister, or Curate, shall make or cause to be made a Catalogue of all the Books, and deliver the same, as aforesaid, within Six Months after he shall receive such Library.

And to prevent any Embezelment of Books upon the Death or Removal of any Incumbent, Be it also Enacted by the Authority aforesaid, That immediately after the Death or Removal of any Incumbent, Rector, Vicar, Minister, or Curate, the Library belonging to such Parish or Place shall be forthwith shut up, and Locked, or otherwise Secured by the Churchwarden or Churchwardens for the time being, or by such Person or Persons as shall be Authorized or Appointed by the proper Ordinary, or Arch-Deacon respectively, so that the same shall not be Opened again, till a new Incumbent, Rector, Vicar, Minister, or Curate shall be Inducted or Admitted into the Church of such Parish or Place.

Provided always, That in case the Place where such Library is or shall be kept shall be used for any Publick Occasion for Meeting of the Vestry, or otherwise, for the dispatch of any Business of the said Parish, or for any other Publick Occasion, for which the said Place hath been Ordinarily used, the Place shall nevertheless be made use of as formerly for such Purposes, and after such Business dispatched, shall be again forthwith Shut and Lockt up, or otherwise Secured, as is before directed.

And be it also further Enacted by the Authority aforesaid, That for the better Preservation of the Books belonging to such Libraries, and that the Benefactions given towards the same may appear, a Book shall be kept within the said Library for the Entring and Registring of all such Benefactions, and such Books as shall be given towards the same, and therein the Minister, Rector, Vicar, or Curate of the said Parish or Place, shall Enter or cause to be fairly Entred such Benefaction, and an Account of all such Books as shall from time to time be given, and by whom given.

And for the better governing the said Libraries, and preserving of the same, It is hereby further Enacted by the Authority aforesaid, That it shall and may be Lawful to and for the proper Ordinary, together with the Donor of such Benefaction (if Living) and after the Death of such Donor, for the proper Ordinary alone, to make such other Rules and Orders concerning the same, over and above, and besides, but not contrary to such as the Donor of such Benefaction shall in his discretion judge fit and necessary ; Which said Orders and Rules so to be made, shall, from time to time, be Entred in the said Book, or some other Book to be prepared for that Purpose, and kept in the said Library.

And it is further Enacted and Declared by the Authority aforesaid, That none of the said Books shall in any case be Alienable, nor any Book or Books that shall hereafter be given by any Benefactor or Benefactors shall be Alienated without the Consent of the proper Ordinary, and then only when there is a Duplicate of such Book or Books ; And that in case any Book or Books be taken or otherwise lost out of the said Library, it shall and may be Lawful to and for any Justice of Peace within the County, Riding or Division, to Grant his Warrant to Search for the same, and in case the same be found, such Book or Books so found shall immediately, by Order of such Justice, be restored to the said Library ; Any Law, Statute or Usage to the contrary in any wise notwithstanding.

Provided always, That nothing in this Act contained shall extend to a Publick Library lately Erected in the Parish of *Rygate* in the County of *Surry*, for the Use of the Freeholders, Vicar, and Inhabitants of the said Parish, and of the Gentlemen and Clergymen, Inhabiting in Parts thereto adjacent ; the said Library being Constituted in another manner than the Libraries Provided for by this Act.

London, Printed by *Charles Bill*, and the Executrix of *Thomas Newcomb*, deceas'd ; Printers to the Queens most Excellent Majesty. 1709.

33. THE FIRST PUBLIC LIBRARIES ACT, 1709
An Act for the preservation of parochial libraries, stimulated by the activities of Thomas Bray and the SPCK.

34. HEREFORD CATHEDRAL LIBRARY
The most famous chained library in Britain. The stalls, a development of the mediaeval lectern, date from 1611, and were copied from those in Duke Humphrey's Library at the Bodleian, Oxford. *F. C. Morgan, by permission of the Dean and Chapter*

only on deposit of one-quarter more than their value. After Kirkwood's death in 1709, no further libraries were distributed, and since no steps were taken to maintain those already in existence they soon fell into disuse.

In dealing with libraries for the clergy we must not neglect to mention the provision made by the cathedrals when their libraries were eventually re-established after the destruction of the Reformation period. By the early eighteenth century most of the English and Welsh cathedrals had collections of a few thousand volumes for the use of the cathedral clergy and such of the parish clergy as were within reach. Even Presbyterian Scotland had one such library, namely at Dunblane Cathedral, to which in 1688 Robert Leighton, formerly Bishop of Dunblane and Archbishop of Glasgow, bequeathed his own library of 1400 books. When episcopacy in Scotland was abolished in the following year, the library was placed under the care of trustees, for the use of clergy and other students. A special building was provided, and arrangements were made for a librarian to be in daily attendance. In England the Presbyterians had Dr Williams's Library in London, which was founded in 1729 under the will of David Williams, a Presbyterian minister, and which became a centre for the study of Nonconformist history and theology.

The most famous of the English cathedral libraries, though not the most typical, is the chained library at Hereford, which was remodelled in 1611, and in spite of many changes in the intervening years has now been restored to something like its pristine condition. About 1500 books are still chained. Other cathedral libraries tended to be more readily accessible, and since their collections often included not only theology but also a certain amount of more general literature, they occasionally served as reference libraries, and even as lending libraries, for non-classical readers. Dr Johnson and Erasmus Darwin, for example, are known to have borrowed from the cathedral library at Lichfield, and Coleridge from that at Carlisle.

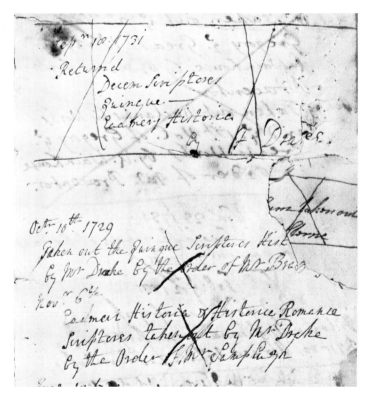

35. PART OF THE BORROWERS' BOOK AT YORK MINSTER LIBRARY
This extract from the Borrowers' Book illustrates the fact that laymen were occasionally permitted to use cathedral libraries. Many of the entries relate to the borrowing of historical works by Francis Drake, surgeon and antiquary, whose book *Eboracum; or the History and Antiquities of York*, was published in 1736. *York Minster Library*

36. JOSEPH PRIESTLEY
Priestley, a Unitarian minister and also a pioneer in the chemistry of gases, played a leading role, during the late eighteenth century, in the establishment of subscription libraries in Warrington, Leeds, and Birmingham. From a contemporary engraving

37. WARRINGTON ACADEMY, 1762
This was one of the best known of the Dissenting academies. Priestley was a tutor there from 1761 to 1767, before taking up a ministry at Leeds, and his house, which still survives, is seen on the left of the picture. The rather splendid iron gates, sadly, found their last resting-place in 1976 in a scrap-dealer's yard. *Cheshire Libraries and Museums*

Gentlemen's Libraries

With the eighteenth century we seem to enter on a new and more modern age – an age more literate, more tolerant, wider in its sympathies, less oppressively concerned with religious issues. Education was advancing apace; new grammar schools continued to be founded; the charity schools established by the SPCK and similar agencies were increasing the provision for elementary education; and the Dissenting academies which came into existence in many parts of the country from the late seventeenth century onwards (initially to train young men for the Nonconformist ministry) were providing a new form of higher education, less hidebound by the classical tradition of the grammar schools and universities, and better adapted to the practical needs of the professional man, the merchant, and the manufacturer. Public lectures on science, which became increasingly popular as the century progressed, added to the general enlightenment.

Newspapers and periodicals now multiplied on every hand, and in spite of heavy taxation were now widely circulated, especially through the coffee houses, which throughout this century played an important role in the dissemination of news and information. Coffee-house life in the capital in the later years of Queen Anne has been immortalised by Steele and Addison in the pages of the *Tatler* and the *Spectator*. The increasing number of cultural clubs and societies – literary, scientific, antiquarian, musical, artistic, and so forth – also contributed to the diffusion of knowledge. Debating societies became common from mid-century onwards, and the last quarter of the century saw the rise of the 'literary and philosophical societies' – a title in which the word 'philosophical' had reference primarily to natural philosophy, i.e. the study of the natural sciences. The famous Lunar Society of Birmingham, which was founded about 1775, and included such distinguished figures as Erasmus Darwin, Richard Lovell Edgeworth, Josiah Wedgwood and Joseph Priestley, was the forerunner of these societies, taking its name from the fact that the members met at the time of full moon in order to make the homeward journey easier. The prototype of the 'lit. and phils.', however, was the Manchester Literary and Philosophical Society, which was founded in 1781 and was famous in its early years for the scientific work of John Dalton.

It will be noted that these developments were by no means confined to London. Many provincial towns, such as Birmingham, Manchester, Liverpool, Leeds, Newcastle and Glasgow, were growing rapidly in wealth and population at this period, and the commercial and industrial leaders of these communities were more and more demanding, and taking steps to provide, the cultural amenities of civilised life.

A very significant development was the advent of the novel, which in the hands of Defoe, Richardson and Fielding now emerged as an important literary form, and quickly attracted readers, especially among women of the leisured middle classes – so much so, indeed, that women novel readers became a favourite subject of parody. The London bookseller James Lackington, however, sprang to their defence. In 1791 he wrote:

> Ladies now in general read, not only novels, although many of that class are excellent productions, and tend to polish both the heart and the head; but they also read the best books in the English language, and many read the best works in various languages; and there are some thousands of ladies, who frequent my shop, that know as well what books to choose, and are as well acquainted with works of taste and genius, as any gentleman in the kingdom, notwithstanding they sneer against novel readers, etc.

This passage illustrates the growing demand among lay people, and particularly among the middle classes, for access to literature of all kinds, both religious and secular. Unfortunately, though books were now smaller and more convenient in format than the great folios of the sixteenth and seventeenth centuries, they were still expensive. At the time Lackington was writing, a quarto work cost a guinea, an octavo 10s or 12s, and a duodecimo 4s a volume, and even the lowest of these figures would represent several pounds in modern currency. The answer was found in the private or commercial subscription library.

The idea of joining together to subscribe for books first appears at Norwich in the seventeenth century, where the old town library, having fallen into a state of complete decay, was in 1656 reconstituted as 'a public library for the common good of students', with a subscription of 12d per quarter, though it was not till 1716 that subscribers were allowed to borrow books. About this latter date a number of parochial libraries in the eastern counties were established, or re-established, on this principle: at Wisbech, for example, in 1712, 'some of the Neighbouring Clergy and Gentlemen, considering the Advantage of Parochial Libraries, formed themselves into a Club or Society, and agreed annually to contribute Twenty Shillings each to buy books'.

The typical 'gentlemen's subscription library' of the late eighteenth and nineteenth centuries, however, was quite independent of the old town and parochial libraries. The earliest examples were in Scotland –

38. THE LYCEUM NEWSROOM AND LIBRARY, LIVERPOOL
The Liverpool Library, founded in 1758, moved in 1803 to this handsome classical
building in Bold Street, and took the new name of the Lyceum. The illustration is
from a drawing by G. and C. Pyne, 1839. *Liverpool City Libraries*

39. BRISTOL CITY
LIBRARY, 1785
This building in King
Street was erected in 1740
to house the library given
to the city by Robert Redwood in 1615. In 1773 it
was handed over, along with
the books, to a subscription
library known as the Bristol
Library Society. The Cor-
poration resumed posses-
sion in 1855, and the building eventually became the
home of the city's Central
Library.
Avon County Library

40. BRISTOL LIBRARY SOCIETY – MEMBERS' REGISTER
In the absence of free public libraries, subscription libraries were of great value to the scholar. In the 1790s both Coleridge and Southey made use of the Bristol Library Society, and their signatures may be seen in this extract from the Members' Register. Another name of interest is that of the physician Thomas Beddoes, who conducted at Clifton a 'Pneumatic Institute' for the treatment of disease by the inhalation of gases. *Avon County Library*

the Society Library of Dumfries (founded about 1745), the Public Library at Kelso (1751), and the Ayr Library Society (1762). On the library at Kelso the *Statistical Account of Scotland* reported in 1794:

> A public library, which has existed upwards of forty years, and can now boast of a collection of the best modern authors, being regularly supplied with every publication of merit; together with a coffee house supplied with the London, Edinburgh and Kelso newspapers, have contributed to render them [the higher classes of inhabitants] not less intelligent than agreeable. The proprietors of the library have lately resolved to erect a neat elegant house for the books, and for the accommodation of the librarian.

The phrase 'every publication of merit' is worth noting, for it neatly sums up the ambition of all eighteenth-century subscription

41. THE MAIN HALL OF THE
BEDFORD GENERAL LIBRARY
Something of the elegance and comfort
typical of the gentlemen's subscription
library is conveyed by this sketch of the
main hall of the Bedford General Library,
erected in 1836. The drawing, by Harold
Town, shows the hall as it was in 1932,
four years before being taken over by the
Bedford Public Library.
Bedfordshire County Library

libraries. They did not aim at comprehensiveness: they excluded
purely professional literature on the one hand, and ephemeral fiction
on the other. The emphasis, therefore, was upon what was commonly
called 'polite literature' – belles lettres, history, biography, travel,
science, and such fiction as was considered to be of literary merit.

In England the prototype of the gentlemen's subscription library
was the Liverpool Library, which was founded in 1758, and was widely
imitated especially in the northern part of the country. Further south
progress was slower, but subscription libraries were launched at
Bristol in 1772, at Birmingham in 1779, and at Norwich in 1784.
The Bristol and Norwich libraries both took over, by agreement, the
old town libraries, which were not restored to public ownership until
the Public Libraries Acts were adopted in the mid-nineteenth century.
London, always laggardly in public library provision, had two
subscription libraries only when the eighteenth century ended. The
famous and still continuing London Library was a latecomer,
founded on the initiative of Thomas Carlyle in 1841.

The typical eighteenth-century subscription library was a fairly
small-scale enterprise – a collection of a few thousand volumes in

Rules and Orders

FOR THE REGULATION OF A

READING SOCIETY OR BOOK CLUB,

AT SHIPSTON-UPON-STOUR, IN THE COUNTY OF WORCESTER.

Established March 25th, 1800.

I.

THAT this Society shall consist of not more than twenty-four members, who shall subscribe on entrance, and annually, not less than ten shillings and sixpence.

II.

That each member shall be at liberty to order any book for this society, he or she may think proper, not exceeding the price of two guineas and an half; provided such book shall be deemed proper for this society, and not wholly profession-al, of which the majority of the members shall judge; and in that case to be wholly paid for by the member ordering the same. And each mem-ber is requested to order annually a book to cost 10s. 6d. or forfeit 10s. 6d. to the funds of the society.

III.

That the members shall receive the books from each other, in order and rotation, as their names shall stand on the list:—the time allowed each member for reading of a large quarto volume shall be fourteen days; for small quartos, ten days; octavos, eight days; and others, one week each; and if longer detained, to forfeit three pence per week for each volume, and so in proportion, which shall be added to the fund of this society.

IV.

That a meeting of this society shall be held once a year, when all the books so ordered by the members shall be sold to the best bidders. Each book shall be put up by or for the person or-dering the same, at half price, when the cost price was twenty shillings or under;—if above, then at two thirds of the cost price; and if no higher bidder shall be found, such person shall be obliged to take to, and pay for, what books he so ordered, after these rates.

V.

That in case the annual subscriptions of ten shillings and sixpence each, with the money raised by sale of the books in manner aforesaid, and by forfeits, shall be insufficient to pay for the books, and other necessary expences of this society, then an equal subscription shall be made, to make up good the deficiency.

VI.

That in case any damage shall be done by a subscriber to any society-book while in his cus-tody (beyond common and reasonable wear) such subscriber shall pay for such damage, or furnish another book of the same sort, in good condition.

VII.

That the books of this society shall be procured in boards, and not bound.

VIII.

That some proper person shall be appointed to furnish the books for this society, and such books, when read, shall be deposited until the end of the year with Mr. Colbourne, who shall have the care thereof, and send them on.

IX.

That for the care and trouble attending this business a reasonable allowance shall be made, over and besides the profits on the purchase of the books.

X.

That at the general annual meeting the mem-bers shall dine together; and in default, non-at-tendants, gentlemen shall pay 5s. and ladies 3s. each for their ordinary; and at such meeting any new members may be elected, who shall be ap-proved of by a majority of the old members then present; and any new rules and regulations for the better ordering of this society may at such general meeting be made.

XI.

That no society-book shall be lent by, or used out of, the families of the respective subscribers, under a forfeiture of two shillings and sixpence for each offence.

XII.

That all books which may be ordered into this society prior to the annual meeting, shall be con-tinued in circulation for the use of the members, until the same shall have circulated to each mem-ber, according to the rules of the society.

Shipston-on-Stour, April, 1828.

WARD, PRINTER, STRATFORD.

Concordia Difcors.——HOR.

43. 'THE COUNTRY
BOOK CLUB'
An illustration from an anonymous satirical poem published
under this title in 1788. It
describes a book club, apparently in an Essex village,
where the members meet 'to
dispute, to fight, to plead, to
smoke, to drink, do anything
but read'. The original, in-
terestingly, was etched by
Thomas Rowlandson.

hired premises, quite often over a bookshop with the bookseller
acting as librarian. Membership was restricted to the shareholders,
who commonly paid a guinea entrance fee and five or six shillings a
year subscription. The clientèle included gentry, clergy, professional
men, manufacturers and well-to-do tradespeople. The control of the
library was in the hands of a committee, and the librarian functioned
merely as custodian for a fee of about £10 a year. In the following
century the scale of provision grew, and many libraries in the larger
provincial cities procured handsome premises of their own and
became rather exclusive establishments. By 1850 the Liverpool
Library, which was the largest in the country and was now known as
the Lyceum, had a stock of 36,760 volumes.

A simpler and related form of organisation, appropriate to small
groups, was the book club or reading society. Characteristically such
an organisation made no attempt to build a permanent collection, the
books being either sold or divided among the members when they
had served their turn. The general plan was to meet monthly to share
out the books and decide on new purchases, and these regular
meetings often served a social as well as a literary purpose. In some
cases indeed, as in the Country Book Club here illustrated, the social
element predominated.

The story of commercial subscription libraries (generally known as
circulating libraries) closely parallels that of the private subscription
libraries. They had their precursors in late seventeenth-century
London, where a number of booksellers made a practice of hiring out

44. BOOKPLATE OF JOSEPH BARBER OF NEWCASTLE

In 1746 Barber established Newcastle's first commercial circulating library, which continued in business until 1785. This bookplate, which had the distinction of being engraved by Thomas Bewick, must belong to its later years. In 1757 Barber was charging borrowers 3d a week, 2s 6d a quarter, or 10s a year. *Newcastle upon Tyne Libraries*

45. HALL'S CIRCULATING LIBRARY AT MARGATE, 1789

As this and the succeeding picture illustrate, many of the major circulating libraries, especially in the spas and holiday resorts, sought to match or even outdo the amenities offered by the gentlemen's subscription libraries. One palatial establishment here shown was obviously an assembly room and promenade as well as a library. *Radio Times Hulton Picture Library*

surplus volumes, but the first unmistakeable example was the lending library established in the High Street of Edinburgh by Allan Ramsay, bookseller, poet, and wigmaker, in 1725. In the second half of the century the bookseller's circulating library became common in London, in the larger provincial towns, and in the spas and watering places. The arrangements made were similar to those afterwards adopted by such well known establishments as Mudie's, Smith's, Boot's, and the Times Book Club, but these national enterprises were all later innovations – from the mid-nineteenth century onwards.

The better circulating libraries offered a range of literature similar to that offered by private subscription libraries, but in general there was a greater emphasis upon entertaining literature, and some, like the 2d subscription libraries of the present century, concentrated almost entirely upon novels and romances. It was this kind of provision which led to the famous denunciation of the circulating library, in Sheridan's *The Rivals*, as 'an evergreen tree of diabolical knowledge'.

46. THE MARINE LIBRARY AT HASTINGS, 1821
The conduct of a circulating library was normally combined with a book-selling business, often also (as in some modern instances) with the sale of stationery, perfumery, and other articles. J. Barry, proprietor of the Marine Library, also published *The Hastings Guide*, from which this illustration is taken.

Working Men's Libraries

A striking early example of library provision for working men is the subscription library formed in 1741 at Leadhills, a lead mining community in the hills of Lanarkshire. Thanks to the widespread system of parish schools which had been created during the seventeenth and eighteenth centuries, the rural inhabitants of Scotland were better educated than their English counterparts, and the Leadhills miners, because of enlightened management, had the additional advantage of a short working day (six hours underground) and relatively high wages. It was in these circumstances that they set on foot the Leadhills Reading Society – the first fully-fledged secular subscription library in Great Britain. All the founder members were miners except the minister and the schoolmaster. They paid an entrance fee of 3s and an annual subscription of 2s, and were allowed to take out six books at a time. They met once a month to exchange their books, the proceedings opening with prayer. The local gentry supported the library with gifts and subscriptions.

Though this was a secular library, the keen interest in theology so long characteristic of the Scots was reflected in the fact that most of the early books purchased were religious, including such classics as Henry Scougal's *Life of God in the Soul of Man*, and Hugo Grotius's *Truth of the Christian Religion*. History came next in popularity, but otherwise the humanities were somewhat sparsely represented. Other subjects at this period included mineralogy, chemistry, astronomy and natural history.

This library became well known, and in the nineteenth century, when the rule restricting membership to those working in Leadhills was relaxed, it attracted members from as far away as Glasgow and Edinburgh. One of the Edinburgh members was Dr John Brown, who in his *Horae Subsecivae* writes of the inhabitants of Leadhills with awe and admiration:

> The people are thoughtful and solid, great readers and church-goers. They have a capital library . . . . We have been greatly struck with the range of subjects and of authors in this homely catalogue; and it is impossible to think with anything but respect of the stout-hearted, strong-brained men who, after

being in the bowels of the earth all day, sat down to wrestle
with John Owen or Richard Baxter, or dream of heaven and
holiness with Scougall and Leighton, or refresh themselves
with Don Quixote, the Antiquary, the Fool of Quality, and
Daubuisson on 'The Basalts of Saxony' – besides eviscerating,
with the help of Jonathan Edwards and Andrew Fuller, their
own gloomy and masculine theology as mercilessly as they did
the stubborn galena and quartz.

The example of Leadhills was followed in 1756 by the neighbouring
village of Wanlochhead in Dumfriesshire, and in 1792 by another
Dumfriesshire village, Westerkirk. Here, too, the library served the
needs of a well-to-do mining community – lead miners at Wanlochhead, antimony miners at Westerkirk, for this latter village had the
distinction of possessing the only antimony mine in Great Britain.

England can offer no real parallel to these Scottish libraries, though
we do hear of working men's subscription libraries at Kendal and
Birmingham in the closing years of the eighteenth century. Both in
England and in Scotland, it is in general true that the main development of libraries for the working people comes in the nineteenth
century, and is associated with that great series of changes which it
has been customary to call the Industrial Revolution. These changes –
demographic, social, economic, technological – were already well
under way before the eighteenth century ended. A major factor was
the rapid expansion of population, and especially the concentration
of population in the large manufacturing and commercial centres,

which within a short space of time converted cities such as Manchester, Liverpool, Birmingham, Leeds and Glasgow from small market towns to thriving metropolises. Unfortunately, however, this inordinately rapid growth produced slum conditions which persisted for nearly a century, bringing in their wake serious problems of health, housing, and education.

In this new setting, just at a time when technological developments in industry and agriculture were calling for a better educated work force, and when economists such as Adam Smith and T. R. Malthus were actually arguing the case for universal education, the institutions which had hitherto sufficed for popular education – the grammar schools, the private schools, the charity schools – obviously needed reinforcement.

At the level of child education the major reinforcement came from the development, early in the nineteenth century, of a new type of denominational elementary school based on the use of the 'monitorial' system, i.e. the system in which the teacher taught a group of monitors, and each monitor taught a group of pupils. The story of these schools, which spread rapidly under the auspices both of the Church of England and of the Nonconformist churches, is a familiar one: it

49. STOCKPORT SUNDAY SCHOOL, 1835
This factory-like building accommodated about 5000 scholars, many of them adults.

was the application of mass production methods to education. A supplementary education, or in many cases a substitute education, was provided by the Sunday schools, which had their beginnings in the late eighteenth century and soon became almost universal. These schools, whose teachers were voluntary and unpaid, customarily had two sessions each Sunday, and many children were indebted to them for their first introduction to reading and elementary education. They played a specially important role in Wales and in industrial Lancashire and Yorkshire. One great school in Stockport had about 5000 scholars. The Education Census for England and Wales in 1851 was able to report that 'very few children are completely uninstructed;

50. TEACHING IN THE ADULT SCHOOLS
The opening page of *Lessons for the Instruction of Adults, or, an Introduction to the Reading of the Holy Scriptures*, published by the Walton-le-Dale Adult School Society, 2nd edition, 1817. Walton-le-Dale, a small industrial township near Preston, had at this time eight adult schools with nearly 400 scholars.

LESSONS for ADULTS.

IN teaching the 23 following lessons * of words of one syllable, the utmost pains should be taken, that every word be made perfectly familiar to the learner, as he proceeds: if the lessons are passed over, as often happens in the general run of schools, in a slovenly and careless manner, a load of toil and tedium is laid up; and the learner, conscious of his imperfect and slow progress, and puzzled and embarrassed by every lesson, feels dissatisfied and disgusted with his teacher, his school, and his book.

Each lesson should be read, 1st, by Previous Spelling; i. e. resolving a word into letters; thus, *a-n-d, and;* observing to pause an instant between each letter, and pronouncing aloud the last letter of each word.

2d, Word by Word; omitting the process of spelling.

3d, By Spelling off Book; thus, the teacher says *and,* the learner repeats *and,* and then spells it, *a-n-d;* pausing an instant between each letter, and pronouncing aloud the last letter of the word; but does not repeat the word after it is spelt.

The learner should be taught to articulate every letter and word, correctly, and in a slow, distinct, and audible manner.

No lesson should be passed over before it is learnt, nor dwelt upon after it is learnt. The teacher should always, even from the beginning, read or spell, &c. in turn with his class, as its exemplar.

FIRST CLASS.

Monosyllabic Spelling.

LESSON I.

be he me we up
can for dig ask
vex joy quit zeal

* These lessons contain almost every important monosyllable in the Bible: each of the two first contain all the letters in the alphabet.

Dr George Birkbeck, a Quaker physician, played a leading role in the mechanics' institute movement. In 1800, as Professor of Natural Philosophy at Anderson's Institution, Glasgow, he was so impressed by the interest and intelligence of workmen helping to make models for his lectures that he started a special 'mechanics' class', which later developed, in 1823, into the Glasgow Mechanics' Institution. In this picture from the title-page of Timothy Claxton's *Hints for Mechanics* (1839), Birkbeck is seen talking to a group of operatives.

nearly all, at some time or another of their childhood, see the inside of a schoolroom, though some do little more'.

In Wales and the industrial north many Sunday schools catered for adults as well as children, but in the main the provision for the education of adults was made through separate institutions, and especially through the adult schools and the mechanics' institutes. The adult school movement was primarily concerned with literacy education, its first simple objective being to teach the poor to read the Holy Scriptures, but in course of time the instruction was expanded to include other forms of elementary education. The first adult school was started in Nottingham in 1798, but the main movement began in Bristol in 1812, and it was from this centre that the work spread to other parts of the country.

The mechanics' institutes, which had their beginnings in Edinburgh, Glasgow and London in the early 1820s, and became especially numerous in the industrial areas, aimed initially at a more sophisticated audience, their purpose being aptly summed up in the rules of the London Mechanics' Institution as 'the instruction of the Members in the principles of the Arts they practise, and in the various branches of science and useful Knowledge'. This purpose they sought to achieve by systematic courses of lectures, especially in science, and by the establishment of a library and museum. Before long it became plain that what was being offered was above the heads of most working men, and it became necessary to simplify. The systematic lecture courses gave way to programmes of miscellaneous general interest lectures, and in most institutes the main emphasis of the teaching work shifted to classes in which more elementary instruction could be provided, from the three Rs upwards. The library,

For the third Volume of the Register of Arts & Sciences

Drawn by L Hebert   Eng.d by J Westley

A Perspective View of the

London Mechanics' Institution,

established the 24 of Dec. 1823 for the purpose of

INCREASING the KNOWLEDGE, REFINING the TASTE,

& eliciting the Genius of the Artisans of

(L O N D O N.)

52. THE LONDON MECHANICS' INSTITUTE

This was the parent institute south of the Border, and was established in 1823. George Birkbeck, by this time a physician in London, was again deeply involved, and the institute eventually became Birkbeck College, a college of London University catering specially for adult students.

Opposite:

53. STALYBRIDGE MECHANICS' INSTITUTE

Hundreds of mechanics' institutes were founded, in towns and villages throughout the country. Not all were as grand as the London one. At Stalybridge, from 1825 to 1842, the institute occupied this garret room, which afterwards, as the photograph shows, became a tailor's workshop.

however, remained a central feature: in 1849 Samuel Smiles, speaking of the Yorkshire institutes, declared that it was 'necessary to have a library to keep the institution together'.

Apart from the adult schools and the mechanics' institutes, there were a number of more radical movements – political clubs, cooperative societies, Chartist societies and the like – which contributed in some measure to working-class adult education, but the sum total of their contribution was not very great. More significant was the cheap literature movement which began in the 1820s with the object of providing cheap and wholesome literature for the working classes, free from religious or other propaganda. The Society for the Diffusion of Useful Knowledge, launched in 1826 under the leadership of Henry Brougham, took the lead in this task, its publications including such series as the *Library of Useful Knowledge*, the *Library of Entertaining Knowledge*, the *Penny Magazine*, and the *Penny Cyclopaedia*. Eventually in 1846 the failure of an ambitious *Biographical Dictionary* brought about the Society's downfall. Other pioneers were Charles Knight, who also acted as publisher to the SDUK; the brothers William and Robert Chambers, who launched *Chambers's Journal*, *Chambers's Encyclopaedia*, and many other educational publications; and a little later John Cassell, whose *Popular Educator* was published in 1852–54 and endlessly reprinted. All these were providing the reading material which was so

vital if the reading skills so painfully and often so imperfectly acquired were to be consolidated.

One way and another, it seems that by about 1840 something like three-quarters of the adult population had some ability to read, and about three-fifths some knowledge of writing, but that those with any competence in arithmetic, or more advanced subjects, still numbered less than half. There were, however, great differences between social groupings and of course between individuals; and many working men – especially craftsmen – were in every sense well educated. It is not necessary, in this connection, to think of outstanding personalities such as Francis Place the London tailor or Thomas Cooper the Gainsborough shoemaker: Elizabeth Gaskell points out in her novel *Mary Barton* (1848) that the textile workers of Lancashire included many men of uncommon accomplishments:

> In the neighbourhood of Oldham there are weavers, common handloom weavers, who throw the shuttle with unceasing sound, though Newton's 'Principia' lie open on the loom . . . There are botanists among them, equally familiar with either the Linnaean or the Natural system, who know the name and habitat of every plant within a day's walk from their dwellings . . . There are entomologists, who may be seen with a rude-looking net, ready to catch any winged insect, or a kind of dredge, with which they rake the green and slimy pools; practical, shrewd, hard-working men, who pore over each new specimen with real scientific delight.

Though we must not underestimate the wretched housing conditions, the dirt, disease and drunkenness, which still characterised life in the new industrial areas, and which were so graphically described by Engels in his *Condition of the Working Classes in England in 1844*, it would be a great mistake to suppose that the entire working class was sunk in poverty and ignorance.

Most of the library provision made for the working classes was philanthropic in character, and much of it was specifically religious in its associations. Church, chapel and Sunday school libraries were to be found by mid-century in almost every town and village, dispensing for the most part the pious publications of the Religious Tract Society and the Society for Promoting Christian Knowledge: the former Society alone distributed more than 4000 libraries in Great Britain between 1832 and 1849. In many rural areas the clergy were active in promoting village lending libraries, sometimes with a nominal subscription, e.g. 1d a week. Such, for example, was the library established in 1807 by Francis Wrangham, Vicar of

Hunmanby, near Scarborough:

> I have lately founded a small parish library, which I keep in my
> vestry, consisting of the twelve volumes of the Christian Society's
> Tracts, the Cheap Repository Tracts, the Cottage Library, two
> volumes, the Pilgrim's Progress, Gilpin's Lives of Truman and
> Atkins, Doddridge's Gardiner, Susan Gray, Lucy Franklin,
> etc. etc., under an idea that the lower classes delight more in
> *concretes* than in *abstracts*; or (in other words) that sermons are
> less read than tales.

An unusual type of library which attracted much attention was the
itinerating library introduced in East Lothian in 1817 by a Haddington merchant, Samuel Brown. From his own resources, and from the
contributions of his friends, Brown provided boxes of fifty books
to be placed 'in every village or hamlet where a librarian could be
found', and to be exchanged every two years. At least half the books
were religious, the rest being popular works of general interest. The
scheme operated for some years with considerable success, but
attempts to introduce the plan in other parts of Scotland proved less
satisfactory.

HINTS.

1. When a Book is got out, it ought to be read regularly through, not reading pieces here and there as the fancy or caprice may dictate, by which the connection is lost, and time spent to little or no purpose.

2. When you sit down to read, let it be with a desire to be instructed rather than entertained. If you do so, you will soon find entertainment in the instruction; but if you accustom yourselves to throw a book aside because it is not so entertaining as you would wish, there is no great hope of you ever becoming wise by reading.

3. Do not weary to get to the end of a Book, or to a certain part of which you already know something.—If the mind is allowed thus to anticipate what is to follow, you will be tempted to hurry over, and thus lose the benefit of all that goes before.

4. Endeavour to understand all that you read. Read a sentence over and over again, rather than lose its meaning.—It is better to read little and profit by it, than to read much without benefit. When, therefore, the mind begins to wander, or sleep steals upon the senses, it is time to stop.

5. Before again beginning to read, endeavour to recollect the connection of what was read formerly; going back, if necessary, for a page or two, and reading a few lines at the beginning of the different paragraphs, till you furnish your memory with the subject, and then go on. Frequently converse on the subject of the book you read with your friends and companions. You will find it very useful to make extracts of the interesting passages of a book after you have read it.

6. Do not allow your book to infringe on your other duties. Remember your master's time is not yours, and therefore rob him not of it without his consent. Beware even of encroaching too far on your hours of rest, or neglecting the daily duties of meditation and prayer. Ask God's blessing on all you read, and endeavour to turn it to profit in your daily practice, following the good and avoiding the evil examples recorded for your instruction. Thus, it is hoped, you will not only increase in knowledge, but, by the blessing of God, " become wise unto salvation."

In 1831 a similar scheme was inaugurated in South Wales under the auspices of the Society for the Improvement of the Working Men of Glamorgan, with headquarters at Cowbridge. Though not specifically religious this was operated through the local clergy, and had a strong establishment air about it, its main object being to counter agitation and unrest among the agricultural workers of the region by diffusing 'a general knowledge of the circumstances on which the well-being of the community depends' – including 'the institution of property, the principles which regulate the price of labour, and the manner in which that price is affected by machinery'. The agricultural labourers, alas, do not seem to have been impressed by this concern for their welfare, and the scheme was short-lived.

Secular libraries for working people, variously known as Working Men's Libraries, Mechanics' Libraries, Tradesmen's Libraries, and the like, became increasingly common from the 1820s onwards. Operating usually on a very small subscription – perhaps 6d, 1s, or 1s 6d per quarter – they were usually dependent in some measure on philanthropic support, provided either by direct gift or by the device of honorary membership. Outstanding examples were the Sheffield Mechanics' and Apprentices' Library, founded in 1823, the Liverpool Mechanics' and Apprentices' Library, inaugurated in the following year, and the Edinburgh Mechanics' Subscription Library which dated from 1825. The Sheffield library steadfastly refused to admit to its shelves 'novels, plays and works subversive of the Christian religion', and acquired some notoriety by rejecting even the works of Shakespeare and Scott. The Liverpool library, however, was more liberal in its policy, excluding only works of an immoral tendency; and in Edinburgh, the largest of the three, with by mid-century a collection of nearly 18,000 volumes, two-thirds of the issues were fiction and light literature.

J. W. Hudson, whose pioneer work, *The History of Adult Education* (1851), provides us with much valuable information concerning nineteenth-century libraries, could barely restrain his enthusiasm for these institutions. Of that at Liverpool he wrote:

> In this humble seminary the mind of the working-man, the journeyman baker, and the dock labourer, receive cultivation, not in reading the latest accounts of misdemeanours and local calamities, but in imbibing instruction and high gratification from the perusal of select and valuable works, whether they lead him with the traveller across the pathless tracts of ocean, or cheer and console him with moral sketches of human nature.

At the same time he reveals how modest was the scale of their operations, and the accommodation at their disposal. The Edinburgh library, which charged 1s 6d a quarter, was 'located in the basement of a large house, in a back street, in the centre of Edinburgh . . . attained by a back stair dimly lighted, and ever thronged', while the Liverpool library, which charged 1d for each visit, occupied the upper floor of a large warehouse, and was reached 'from a back street by a narrow intricate stair, dimly lighted on winter evenings'. None the less all three libraries survived until rate-aided libraries came to take their place in the second half of the century

The most familiar source of books for the working man, however, was unquestionably the mechanics' institute. By mid-century there were some 700 institutes in the country, including about thirty in Wales and about fifty in Scotland; and there was also a host of rather similar organisations – athenaeums, literary societies, mutual improvement societies and the like. Almost every one of these organisations had its library, not a very large library, or a very good library, but still a library. In general the mechanics' institute libraries tended to concentrate at the outset, like the Sheffield Mechanics' and Apprentices' Library, on serious literature, and especially scientific literature, but by 1850 fiction, biography, travel and general literature were the main staple of most institute libraries, with fiction the most popular of all.

One of the largest libraries was that of the Manchester Mechanics' Institute, which in 1850 numbered 12,000 volumes. Though fiction

NORTHAMPTON MECHANICS' Institute.

The Members of the Northampton Mechanics' Institute are respectfully informed
that the

Library Of Circulation,

AND

Reading Room

Of the Institute, Saint Mary's Street,

WILL BE OPENED

On Tuesday, Jan. 8, 1833.

The Reading Room will continue open *every* Night, from Seven till Ten o'Clock (Sundays excepted); the Library of Circulation on *Tuesdays* and *Fridays* only.

No Member can possibly be admitted without producing his Subscription Ticket.

Mercury Office.   G. J. DE WILDE, Secretary.

was now the largest section, it was and had been from the beginning a general library, including science, history, and 'polite literature'. It was open daily, except Sundays, from 10 a.m. to 9.30 p.m., and lending issues reached a peak of 54 volumes per member in 1848. There was also a reading room, with periodicals and a small reference collection; and a newsroom which supplied a wide range of London, provincial and foreign newspapers.

The library of the Chichester Mechanics' Institute led the way in the 1830s in establishing travelling libraries, supplying boxes of books to branch institutions in two neighbouring villages. In the second half of the century this idea was taken up on a larger scale by unions of mechanics' institutes in the North of England.

In many instances institute libraries continued to serve the needs of the public, in the absence of rate-aided public libraries, well into

57. THE WARRINGTON MECHANICS' INSTITUTE PERAMBULATING LIBRARY, 1860
A picture in the *Illustrated London News* showing an interesting horse-drawn anticipation of the modern mobile library. The experiment began about 1858, and seems to have been short-lived.
Cheshire Libraries and Museums

the twentieth century, outstanding examples being Crewe, where the library service was taken over by the local authority only in 1936, and Swindon, where the rate-aided library opened only in 1943.

Even yet we have not mentioned all the various types of libraries which were in some degree open to the public. The fact is that in the absence of a comprehensive public library service practically every social organisation sought to provide its members with books. There were libraries in clubs and pubs, in benefit societies, in cooperative societies, in factories, in coffee houses, even, for a brief space, in London's horse-drawn omnibuses. When agencies such as these are added to those already described – the cathedral and endowed libraries, the libraries of literary and philosophical societies and other learned societies, the libraries of mechanics' institutes and similar bodies, the subscription libraries and book clubs, and the commercial circulating libraries, it is clear that whatever early nineteenth-century Britain lacked it did not lack libraries. But the quality of the provision was very poor, and except for the well-to-do who had large private libraries, or access to a learned library or a good subscription library, the total supply of books was very inadequate. As far as working people were concerned, there was much truth in the evidence given by George Dawson, a well known public lecturer, to the Select Committee on Public Libraries in 1849:

> The fact is, we give the people in this country an appetite to read, and supply them with nothing. For the last many years in England everybody has been educating the people, but they have forgotten to find them any books.

58. BOOKPLATE OF THE KING'S LYNN MECHANICS' INSTITUTE
Norfolk County Library

Further Reading

The most recent account of the history of public libraries in this country is to be found in two works by Thomas Kelly, namely *Early Public Libraries* (Library Association 1966) and *A History of Public Libraries in Great Britain* (Library Association 1973). To these two volumes, on which the text of the present work is in a substantial measure based, we venture to recommend the reader for more detailed references to sources. Two earlier books of great value are W. A. Munford's centenary survey, *Penny Rate: Aspects of British Public Library History, 1850–1950* (Library Association 1951); and W. J. Murison, *The Public Library: its Origins, Purpose and Significance* (Harrap 1955, 2nd edn. 1971). The county library service is briefly but admirably dealt with in K. A. Stockham (ed.), *British County Libraries: 1919–1969* (Deutsch 1969). Scottish developments are carefully described in W. R. Aitken, *A History of the Public Library Movement in Scotland to 1955* (Scottish Library Association, Glasgow 1971). Alec Ellis, *Library Services for Young People in England and Wales, 1830–1970* (Pergamon 1971) is useful throughout.

T. Kelly, *Early Public Libraries*, cited above, is the most comprehensive account of public and semi-public libraries before 1850. See also the early chapters of John Minto, *A History of the Public Library Movement in Great Britain and Ireland* (Allen and Unwin 1932), and for general background Raymond Irwin's *The Origins of the English Library* (Allen and Unwin 1958, published in an enlarged edition as *The English Library: Sources and History* 1966); and the same author's *The Heritage of the English Library* (Allen and Unwin 1964). Edward Edwards's monumental *Memoirs of Libraries* (2v. 1859) is still worth consulting. For the precursors in Scotland see W. R. Aitken, *A History of the Public Library Movement in Scotland to 1955*, cited above.

Mediaeval and early modern libraries are dealt with in J. W. Clark, *The Care of Books* (Cambridge University Press 1901, 2nd edn. 1902); E. A. Savage, *Old English Libraries* (Methuen 1911, repr. 1970); and F. Wormald and C. E. Wright (eds.), *The English Library before 1700* (Athlone Press 1958).

For parochial libraries see Central Council for the Care of Churches, *The Parochial Libraries of the Church of England* (Faith Press 1959); and Paul Kaufman, *Libraries and their Users* (Library Association 1969). This latter work, however, is mainly concerned with subscription and circulating libraries, on which see also Frank Beckwith, 'The Eighteenth-Century

Proprietary Library in England', in *Journal of Documentation*, Vol. III (1947–8); and H. M. Hamlyn, 'Eighteenth-Century Circulating Libraries in England', in *The Library*, 5th. Ser., Vol. I (1947).

Aspects of the early nineteenth century are dealt with in C. B. Oldman, W. A. Munford, and S. Nowell-Smith, *English Libraries, 1800–1850* (Lewis 1958). For the mechanics' institute libraries of this period see Thomas Kelly, *George Birkbeck* (Liverpool University Press 1957); and Mabel Tylecote, *The Mechanics' Institutes of Lancashire and Yorkshire before 1851* (Manchester University Press 1957).

59. JAMES SILK
BUCKINGHAM
From the engraving by
G. T. Doo in Buckingham's
Autobiography (1855).

The Beginnings of the Public Library Service

The Origins

The Public Libraries Act of 1850, which as we have noted is commonly regarded as the starting point of the local public library service, is part of that great body of reforming legislation which began with the Parliamentary Reform Act of 1832. The result, by the end of the century, was not only a complete transformation in our system of central and local government but also a substantial widening of the powers of both. From this latter point of view the Public Libraries Act takes its place alongside the first Factory Act of 1833, the first Public Health Act of 1848, and the first Education Act of 1870. More specifically, public libraries were one of the instruments through which a philanthropic and conscience-stricken middle class sought to alleviate the lot of the poor, and at the same time to inculcate habits of honesty, sobriety, and obedience. From this point of view they are to be grouped with charity schools, adult schools, mechanics' institutes, workingmen's subscription libraries, public parks, public baths and wash-houses, and other enterprises through which an attempt was made to mitigate some of the worst evils of the Industrial Revolution, especially among the urban working class.

For it was to the working class that public library provision was first directed, and at the outset the main emphasis was on social reform rather than upon education. This is clearly seen in the first attempt to secure legislative sanction for public libraries, which was made in the year 1835, and was closely linked with the temperance movement. The lead in the matter was taken by a self-educated Cornishman, James Silk Buckingham, traveller, writer and lecturer, who entered the reformed House of Commons in 1832, and served for five years as member for Sheffield.

The evils of drunkenness have been denounced by moralists since the earliest times, and in this country, in the first half of the eighteenth century, they had become a matter of national concern. This was because of the spread of gin-drinking, following the introduction of cheap home-produced gin during the French wars. The dramatic effects of this indulgence were highlighted in 1751 in William Hogarth's famous engraving 'Gin Lane'. In the same year Henry Fielding, who was a magistrate as well as a novelist, reported that in the capital gin was 'the principal Sustenance (if it may be so called) of more than a hundred thousand People'; and alarm was also expressed in other large towns. Bristol, Manchester, Norwich, Rochester and Salisbury all petitioned Parliament to take action to stop excessive drinking, which was bringing about a 'great Decay of Industry, Piety and Virtue among the common People'. Parliament responded by legislation to strengthen control over the production and sale of spirits, and during the latter part of the eighteenth century the situation gradually improved. It was at this time that the consumption of tea, even among the poorer classes, began to rival that of alcohol. The Industrial Revolution, however, brought new problems, and in the overcrowded working-class areas of the industrial towns drunkenness remained a serious evil.

It is fair to say that drunkenness was not restricted to the poor, or even to the working classes: it was, in fact, a common vice among all classes, and the poor wretch who sought in the ale-house an escape from the squalid slum in which he was compelled to live was perhaps less deserving of censure than the squire or alderman who drank himself under the table every evening. It was not until 1831, the year before Buckingham entered Parliament, that the first national temperance organisation, the British and Foreign Temperance Society, was founded in London. In the previous year the Government had done much to increase drunkenness by removing the tax on beer and abolishing most of the controls on the opening of beer shops.

When in 1834 Buckingham proposed a Select Committee to inquire into 'the extent, causes, and consequences of the prevailing vice of intoxication among the labouring classes of the United Kingdom', he met with considerable ridicule, and was opposed even by the Government. In his speech to the Commons he brought forward evidence from many parts of the country to show the increase of drunkenness, and listed some of the causes, amongst them excessive taxation and excessive labour:

> These two causes operating conjointly, rendered it almost impossible for labouring men to provide themselves with homes of comfort, and therefore the blazing fire and easy chair of the tap-room of the public house, possessed a more powerful attraction for them than an empty hearth, a damp floor, and a cold and comfortless lodging.

60. THE DRUNKARD'S CHILDREN
The artist George Cruikshank was an enthusiastic temperance advocate. This cartoon of about 1840, showing how the drunkard's children are corrupted in the gin shop, provokes comparison with Hogarth's 'Gin Lane'. *Radio Times Hulton Picture Library*

61. 'THE TEMPTATION'
Temperance advocates strongly objected to the common practice of paying out wages in the public house. This engraving, published in 1847, shows the temperate man beset with temptations to drink. *Radio Times Hulton Picture Library*

He also listed the lamentable consequences of this situation:

> Deterioration of the public health, to such a degree that our hospitals and asylums are filled with the victims of intemperance. Increase of pauperism in every parish, so that the poor rates bid fair to exceed the rental of the land. Destruction of public morals, by the brutalization of the old, and the prostitution of the young – the extinction of all honest pride of independence in the men, and the annihilation of all sense of decency in the women – the neglect of wives by their husbands, of children by their parents – and the breaking in sunder all those soft and endearing ties which heretofore were recognized as sacred among the humblest classes in society.

Francis Place, the Charing Cross tailor, a great pioneer in all working-class causes, procured a copy of the printed version of this speech, and filed it away with the comment: 'Containing many gross Exaggerations, falsities and absurdities.' In a pamphlet of his own, published in this same year, and entitled *Improvement of the Working People: Drunkenness – Education*, he contended that drunkenness was in fact on the decline, even among 'the very meanest and least informed' of the labouring classes. However, Buckingham carried his point, and a committee was appointed under his own chairmanship. Place, called upon to give evidence, conceded in answer to a direct question from Buckingham that the establishment of libraries, reading rooms and lectures 'might draw off a number of those who now frequent public houses for the sole enjoyment they afford'.

The question was deliberate. It had been Buckingham's idea from the outset that measures should be taken not only for the control of the liquor trade but also for the provision of constructive alternatives to the public house as places of resort for working people. The Committee's recommendations accordingly included:

> The establishment, by the joint aid of the government and the local authorities, and residents on the spot, of public walks and gardens, or open spaces for athletic and healthy exercises in the open air, in the immediate vicinity of every town, of an extent and character adapted to its population, and of district and parish libraries, museums and reading rooms, accessible at the lowest rate of charge.

In the following year, 1835, Buckingham submitted legislation to implement these recommendations. Significantly, the House refused even to consider further regulations to control the drink trade, but it did consider a bill to secure the provision in all towns of 'Public Walks, Gardens, and Places of Recreation in the Open Air', and another to authorise the erection of 'Public Institutions, to embrace the means of diffusing Literary and Scientific Information, and forming Libraries and Museums in all Towns'. Where necessary funds to cover the initial cost of these institutions could be raised by borrowing, and a sixpenny rate levied to cover the repayment. Future running costs would be met by donations and a small charge to the users. Three times, in successive years, these proposals were brought forward, the third time in the form of a combined bill, but each time they failed: the provision for levying a rate was more than the House could stomach.

All was not lost, however, for these debates did enlist the interest of two men who were to play a leading role in securing the passage of the Act of 1850. One was Joseph Brotherton, MP for Salford and pastor of the Bible Christian Church there. As a total abstainer he was, like Buckingham, keenly interested in temperance and social reform. The other was William Ewart, at this time MP for Liverpool. Though Liverpool-born (his father of the same name was godfather to William Ewart Gladstone), Ewart was Scottish by descent, and he later served for twenty-seven years (1841–68) as MP for Dumfries. In the 'thirties he was primarily interested in training for industrial design, which because of foreign competition was a matter of widespread concern; and the evidence given to the Select Committee on Arts and Manufactures, of which he was chairman in 1835–6, resulted in the first modest steps towards public provision for technical education. From 1837 onwards, initially under the aegis of the Board of Trade, schools of design were established in London and a number of provincial centres.

The Select Committee's recommendations for achieving improved standards of design also included a proposal for the provision of public museums and art galleries, and Ewart now grasped at the idea that public libraries could be a means towards the same end, as well as contributing to the general education and economic betterment of the working classes.

Provision for museums and art galleries came first, under the Museums Act of 1845, which empowered boroughs with a population of 10,000 or more to raise a $\frac{1}{2}$d rate for the establishment of 'museums of art and science', and to make an admission charge not exceeding 1d. This Act was brought forward on the initiative of Ewart and Brotherton, and being presented by Ewart as a means to improve industrial design was readily accepted. Canterbury in 1847, Warrington in 1848, and Salford (at Brotherton's instigation, of course) in 1850, actually took advantage of the Act to establish museums which included books, but this ingenious method of creating a public library was of doubtful legality, and none of these libraries was able, at

62. TWO LIBRARY PIONEERS
Left William Ewart, from a portrait in the possession of the Ewart family.
Right Joseph Brotherton, from a portrait in the Salford City Library.

this stage, to offer a full lending service.

To secure the adoption of a Public Libraries Act proved more difficult. In spite of the Reform Act, the House of Commons was still dominated by the propertied and manufacturing classes, and the economic advantage of public libraries to these classes was not easy to demonstrate. The first step, agreed in March 1849, was the appointment of a Select Committee on Public Libraries, under Ewart's chairmanship, to investigate the current position. In the conduct of this Committee Ewart had invaluable assistance from Edward Edwards, a member of the staff of the British Museum Library, who had already collected a great deal of information on this subject. The result, later in the year, was a fascinating Report reviewing in some detail the existing provision, which the Committee regarded as quite inadequate, and seeking to demonstrate that this provision was much inferior to that made in other countries.

The Committee suggested ways in which existing resources, for example those of the British Museum Library and the university libraries, could be made more readily available, and stressed that if public libraries were to be really useful provision must be made for lending and for evening opening. In order to secure more extensive provision the Committee recommended, first, that the Government, which already made grants in aid of elementary schools and schools of design, should also make grants in aid of libraries; and second, that the Museums Act of 1845 should be extended to permit the establishment of libraries. It is noteworthy that the Committee did not suggest assistance from public funds for the provision of books. Given the buildings, it optimistically declared, 'Donations will abundantly supply the books'. This view, so soon to be proved totally wrong, was in line with the current notion of public libraries as philanthropic institutions.

The Public Libraries Act of 1850 was based on these recommendations, except that it made no provision for Government aid. Introduced by Ewart, and supported by Brotherton, it had a difficult passage through the House, and in its final form it was hedged round with restrictions. Borough councils with a population of 10,000 or more were now empowered to spend a $\frac{1}{2}$d rate on the provision of accommodation for a museum and/or library, and the maintenance of the same, but no provision was made for expenditure on books or museum specimens, and the adoption of the Act was subject to the approval of a two-thirds majority in a special poll of ratepayers.

Nineteenth-Century Attitudes

The debates in the House during the passage of the 1850 Act revealed sharp differences of view. Ewart presented the bill as 'calculated to afford the working classes in our populous towns proper facilities for the cultivation of their minds, and the refinement of their tastes in science and art'. He also stressed the motive of economic betterment, arguing that 'the labouring population would be far more advanced if they had such opportunities as were afforded by means of public libraries to the working classes of other countries'.

Brotherton emphasised the educational and moral improvement that would follow from the bill. The opposition of those who objected to additional taxation was, he thought, short-sighted:

> Here were 2,000,000l. a year paid for the punishment of crime, yet Hon. Gentlemen objected to permitting communities to tax themselves a halfpenny in the pound for the prevention of crime. In his opinion, it was of little use to teach people to read unless you afterwards provided them with books, to which they might apply the faculty they had so acquired. It was well known that the large bulk of the labouring classes had not the means of buying

books of their own; and, therefore, the next best thing was to collect in every town libraries for their free use. He was satisfied that expenditure upon this object would be productive not only of immense moral good, but also of very material public economy, in the long run.

On another occasion he put the point more bluntly: the bill would, he declared, 'provide the cheapest police that could possibly be established'.

R. A. Slaney, MP for Shrewsbury, a keen social reformer, made the same point, and also raised the temperance issue, defending libraries on the ground that

> by encouraging habits which kept the working men from the public house, they lessened the incentives to a dissolute life, and, consequently, to idleness and crime; which cost the country much more than all the libraries they could build under this Bill.

Those who opposed the bill did so usually because they objected to increased taxation, but there were some (even, as Brotherton pointed out, some university members) who were deeply suspicious of any move to spread education among the masses. Thus Sir Robert Inglis, Oxford University, argued that: 'The machinery was clearly adapted, not merely for the purpose of procuring books, but also of creating lecture rooms, which might give rise to an unhealthy agitation.'

R. Spooner, MP for Warwickshire, also voiced the suspicion that 'these libraries might be converted into normal schools of agitation'. Colonel Charles Sibthorp, MP for Lincoln, the Colonel Blimp of this debate, confessed that he himself 'did not like reading at all,' and thought that, 'however excellent food for the mind might be, food for the body was what was now most wanted for the people'.

On one point, however, nearly all members were agreed, and that was that libraries were intended for use of the working classes. This was to be a recurring theme for the next fifty years, and indeed well into the twentieth century. Charles Dickens, at the opening of the Manchester public library in 1852, expressed the hope 'that the books thus made available will prove a source of pleasure and improvement in the cottages, the garrets, and the cellars of the poorest of our people' – a revealing phrase which recalls the vivid descriptions of working-class homes in the same city by Engels eight years earlier. A memorial in favour of a library at Leeds in 1861 drew attention to the

> vast numbers of working men who, for want of some place of proper resort after their day's labour, and in the absence of other available attractions, are compelled to seek for themselves amusements which are unfortunately but too often objectionable,

much poverty and social distress being the necessary results.

The working people themselves accepted this class distinction with a proper humility, and in 1857 a working-class leader in Liverpool warned his fellows that if they were to prove themselves worthy of the great gift their superiors had bestowed upon them (i.e. the public library), they must be prepared to make sacrifices. 'Our leisure hours,' he declared, 'instead of being spent in the tap-room, the singing room and the dancing room, must be given to study, to thought, to perseverance and to industry.'

The Public Libraries Act of 1850 underwent a variety of modifications as the nineteenth century wore on, and the more important of these are indicated below. The procedure for adoption by a poll of the ratepayers, however, was retained until the 'nineties, and in many places there were long and bitter debates as to whether or not a public library should be established. In some centres the proposal was rejected more than once. Bath, Hull, Deptford and St Marylebone rejected it four times, Islington five times. The citizens of Edinburgh, and many parts of London, showed themselves particularly reluctant to assume library responsibilities, and the canny citizens of Glasgow could never be persuaded to adopt the Acts, the procedure being eventually by-passed by a special Act of Parliament.

In the debates about adoption, in town after town throughout the country, we find rehearsed over and over again the arguments for or against public libraries which had taken place in Parliament over the original 1850 Act. As in Parliament, the debate took place mainly among representatives of the middle classes, over the heads of the working classes for whom it was generally agreed that the libraries were intended.

The liberal minded reformers who supported adoption argued that public libraries would make the working classes more sober, more industrious, and more prosperous, thus contributing to the peace, order and prosperity of society at large. The landlords and shopkeepers led the opposition, objecting to paying rates for the benefit of a lot of lazy people with nothing to do but lounge about reading. In not a few instances landlords threatened to put up the rents of their tenants to cover the extra cost. Publicans, booksellers, and proprietors of circulating libraries, were other vested interests often to be found on the opposing side. Libraries were also denounced as spreaders of disease, disrupters of family life, and nurseries of socialism.

The opposition of the publicans illustrates the importance of the temperance issue, which was highlighted in the famous cartoon, *The Rivals*, which formed the frontispiece to the first edition of

63. POSTERS FOR AND
AGAINST ADOPTION
OF THE PUBLIC
LIBRARIES ACTS
AT YORK
After a long struggle,
the Acts were
adopted in 1891 and
the library opened in
1893 in the former
Mechanics' Institute
building.
*North Yorkshire
County Library*

The Committtee for the promotion of a Public Library for York invite attention to the following statements:

What a FREE LIBRARY will cost:

The ENTIRE CHARGE *for every purpose* CANNOT EXCEED THE SUM OF ONE PENNY IN THE £ PER ANNUM *on the rateable value of your house, as this limit is fixed by Act of Parliament.*

Thus,—a Householder whose rent is

£5 a year would pay less than 1¼d. a quarter, or less than 5d. a year.
£7   „   1¾d.   „   7d. „
£10   „   2½d.   „   10d. „
£12   „   3d.   „   1s. „

For this, yourself and family would have
THE FREE USE OF THE LIBRARY.
THE FREE USE OF THE NEWSROOM.
THE RIGHT TO TAKE BOOKS HOME TO READ.

THE (SO CALLED) FREE LIBRARY FOR YORK.

Brother and Sister Ratepayers of York. We shall shortly *be awfully heavily rated,* if you allow this Library Scheme to pass. IF YOU DO NOT WANT IT, GO EARLY TO THE POLL.

Be determined to vote against it.

You must also **look out and check** some of the other Schemes **now proposed by our York Corporation.** You know all about the thin end of the wedge; **don't allow it to be driven home.** As Electors and Ratepayers **we must act for ourselves and for our poorer neighbours,** as many of the Inhabitants are in a most humble condition, and some sick and helpless (**who will not be able to use the Library**), whose burdens and cares are already heavy enough to bear, **yet they will have to pay rates for it.** They look for protection from wrong and it is our duty to afford it to them, therefore

VOTE AGAINST THE LIBRARY SCHEME.

Thomas Greenwood's *Free Public Libraries* in 1886. Greenwood, a publisher of technical literature, had in early life served a brief spell as a branch librarian at Sheffield, and being a keen educationist and temperance reformer he made himself the special advocate of the library movement in the late nineteenth century. His book, which ran through four editions and was followed in 1897 by the first issue of a *Library Year Book*, did much to stimulate the formation of public libraries and to make people aware of the organisational problems involved. The cartoon in his first edition showed side by side the public library, about to be patronised by a couple of earnest and particularly upright citizens, and the Red Lion public house, with a depressed and dissipated-looking character propping up the doorway. Five years later the *Middlesex Courier* put the same thought into words:

> The public house is the ante-room of the gaol, while the library is the doorway of the knowledge which is power – power for success, for prosperity, and for honour. The public house is the high road to perdition; the library the wicket of truth.

The one significant change in public attitudes during this period was the growing importance attached from the late 'sixties onwards to the educational element in library provision. As late as 1861 the Report of the Newcastle Commission on the State of Popular Education was reasonably satisfied with the position, although at that time less than half the children between three and fifteen were enrolled in day schools, but in the larger cities there was growing concern about the lack of educational facilities. This concern was reinforced by a variety of considerations both political and economic.

On the political side the Second Reform Act of 1867 (and the corresponding Scottish Act of 1868) almost doubled the electorate by enfranchising all male householders in the towns and reducing the property qualification for voting in the country districts. It was this Act which led to Robert Lowe's famous pronouncement that 'it will be absolutely necessary to compel our future masters to learn their letters'. The Ballot Act of 1872, and the Third Reform Act of 1884, which enfranchised the rural worker, gave added point to this argument.

The Education Act passed by Gladstone's government in 1870 was the response to this widely felt need. For the first time the principle of universal elementary education, long advocated by reformers, was officially accepted, and local School Boards were established to fill the gaps left by the denominational schools. In Scotland the position in relation to religious education was less controversial, and under the corresponding Scottish Act of 1872 the School Boards took over

Friends & Foes

OF THE

PUBLIC LIBRARY

Working Men, have you compared the Men who ask you to Vote for the Half-penny Rate with those who say don't?

The Mayor and all the Corporation.	Mr. OSMOND, of the Cremorne Tavern,
The whole of the Clergy of all Denominations,	Mr. LEAKER, of the Angel Inn
And all those who usually help in starting and supporting all plans intended to help the WORKING CLASSES,	Mr. Wartenburg, Beerseller,
	Capt. Fitzgerald, of the "Argus,"
	Mr. Reuben Cook, Commercial Traveller,
SAY, "YES."	SAY, "NO."

64. POSTER SUPPORTING THE ADOPTION OF THE PUBLIC LIBRARIES ACTS AT BATH
Public resistance at Bath was particularly obstinate, and it was only after four rejections that the Acts were eventually adopted in 1900. *Avon County Library*

the denominational schools also, and education was made compulsory. In England and Wales compulsion was introduced in 1876 and 1880. The final stage in this epoch-making series of reforms came in 1891 (1893 in Scotland) when elementary education was made free.

On the economic side growing nervousness about foreign competition brought a new emphasis on technical education. The first major government intervention in this field came in 1853 with the creation of the Department of Science and Art, which took over the responsibility for the schools of design and also encouraged the development of technical classes under a great variety of auspices, including mechanics' institutes, cooperative societies, library and museum committees, and evening institutes. This development owed much to the stimulus provided by the Great Exhibition of 1851, but it remained patchy and haphazard. In 1867 the poor showing made by British exhibitors at the Paris Exhibition made it clear that more systematic provision was needed, but it was only after a Select Committee and two Royal Commissions on the subject that Lord Salisbury's government eventually passed the Technical

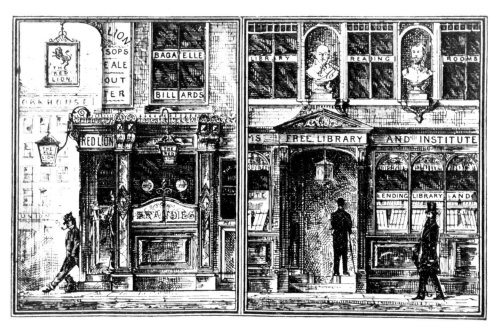

65. THE RIVALS: THE PUBLIC HOUSE AND THE FREE LIBRARY
The famous cartoon by J. Williams Benn in Thomas Greenwood's *Free Public Libraries* (1886)

Instruction Act of 1889, empowering the new county and county borough councils (created in the previous year) to establish Technical Instruction Committees and levy a penny rate for technical and manual instruction. By good luck the Local Taxation Act of 1890 provided additional funds in the form of the 'whisky money', the proceeds of a tax on whisky originally intended to finance the closure of redundant public houses. This additional money continued to be available until 1902.

The 1889 Act became the starting point for a wide development of technical education, with the local authorities rapidly taking over from the mechanics' institutes and other organisations involved. For some years the School Boards and the Technical Instruction Committees operated independently, the former under the direction of the Education Department, the latter under that of the Science and Art Department. It was not until the end of the century that, in England and Wales, the system was unified. The two central government departments were merged in 1899 as the Board of Education, and at the local level rationalisation was achieved by the Education Act of 1902. Under this Act county borough councils were constituted as local education authorities, with responsibility for all publicly maintained elementary, secondary and technical education. County councils were given similar powers, but here the larger non-county borough and urban district councils were given responsibility for elementary education only.

Opposite
66. ADULT EDUCATION IN THE LATE NINETEENTH CENTURY
Above A village evening school, 1862.
Below A practical chemistry class for artisans, 1871.

In Scotland the position was different. Here, by an Act of 1887, technical education developed under the aegis of the School Boards, and it was only in 1918 that these Boards, numbering nearly a thousand, were replaced by fewer than forty county and burgh education authorities.

Against this background it is understandable that the public libraries now began to be thought of not only as instruments of social reform but also as part of a great forward movement in national education, and those who favoured their establishment could argue that they were in fact an investment, which would yield a return in the form of increased prosperity for British industry. The case that Ewart had made for museum provision in 1845 could now be even more plausibly made for libraries. Greenwood, looking back in 1890, came to the conclusion that the 'real impetus' to the development of the library service came with the passing of the Education Act of 1870; and in adoption debates and at library openings there were many to echo the belief expressed by Dr Henry Newton at the opening of the Newcastle upon Tyne Reference Library in 1884. Public libraries would, he declared, 'carry upward and onward the work of the public elementary schools'. Many of them, as we shall see, did so not only by providing reading matter but by themselves engaging, directly or indirectly, in technical and adult education.

An Outline of Library Development to the First World War

Many of the restrictions imposed on the library service by the Act of 1850 were removed or modified by subsequent legislation. In 1855 the permissible rate limit was raised to a penny, and authorities were allowed to spend money not only on library and museum buildings but also on books, newspapers, maps and specimens, and on the provision of schools of science and art. For all these multifarious purposes even a penny rate was clearly insufficient, but it was only in the 1890s, when it became possible to levy separate rates for museums and for technical education, that the full penny rate became available exclusively for library purposes.

The population limit was reduced from 10,000 to 5000 in 1855, and abolished altogether in 1866. This made it necessary to extend the power of adoption not only to boroughs but to other local government units, and eventually, in 1892, it was enacted that a library authority might be either an urban district or a parish not within an urban district, the phrase 'urban district' including both the county boroughs created under the Local Government Act of 1888 and other urban authorities. In London, until the metropolitan borough councils came into existence in 1900, a library authority might be the City, or a district board, or a parish.

The cumbersome and expensive machinery for adoption was for many years a difficulty in the way of those anxious to see libraries established. The procedure for adoption by poll was abandoned in 1855 in favour of adoption by public meeting, but was restored in 1890. A great simplification was achieved when in 1893 urban authorities were permitted to adopt by resolution of the council, but in rural areas the approval of a majority of householders had still to be sought.

Much of the legislation here described related to England and Wales only, but a Public Libraries Act for Scotland was passed in 1853, and although the system of local government there was somewhat different, legislation broadly followed parallel lines. The greatest weakness in all three countries was the absence, after 1866, of any limit on population. This stimulated the growth of numerous small library authorities, many of which, as we shall see, had totally inadequate resources. This weakness was compounded by the subsequent failure to give library powers to the new county authorities, created in England and Wales in 1888 and in Scotland in 1889. It was indeed ludicrous that the Libraries Acts might be adopted by the smallest parish in a county, but the county authority itself was powerless to act. This position persisted, however, until the close of the First World War.

Progress in the development of a library service was at first slow. The first local authority to adopt the Public Libraries Act was the city of Norwich, in 1850, but the decision to erect a special building, providing accommodation not only for the library but for a museum, a school of art, and a private subscription library, meant that service was not actually commenced until 1857. It is interesting to note that the public library committee here specifically included five representatives of the working classes, the first to be appointed being a printer, a weaver, a herbalist, a newsvendor and a hairdresser. This arrangement was continued for some years.

The first authority actually to open a library under the Act was the city of Winchester, which adopted in 1851 and commenced service almost immediately by the simple expedient of taking over the property of the Hampshire Museum, an organisation supported by voluntary funds which included a small collection of books. The problem of premises was solved by converting the governor's house of the former city gaol. The library, tucked away in a 'high and remote part of the

67. MANCHESTER'S FIRST PUBLIC LIBRARY
Left The official opening, 1852. Note the dizzy height of the shelving.
Right An exterior view of the building, originally erected as a 'Hall of Science' for
the followers of Robert Owen.

building', was little used, and long remained subordinate to the
museum. It was not until the 'eighties that a reasonable service
began to be provided.

The first major civic library to be opened was that at Manchester,
which was inaugurated in September 1852 at a ceremony graced by
the presence of the Earl of Shaftesbury, Sir Edward Bulwer Lytton,
Charles Dickens, W. M. Thackeray, John Bright and many other
distinguished figures. A public subscription of nearly £13,000,
including contributions from many thousands of 'hard-working
clerks and artisans', made possible the purchase and adaptation for
library purposes of the former Owenite Hall of Science, and the
expenditure of more than £4000 on an initial selection of books.
Edward Edwards, formerly of the British Museum, was appointed as
the first librarian, and under his care the library at once assumed an
important place in the life of the city. By 1856 it was reported that it
was being extensively used, and by all classes of society.

A similar story can be told of Liverpool, where the public library
opened a month later, in October 1852 – not under the 1850 Act,

but under a special local Act. Here, too, temporary accommodation was used at first, in a former subscription newsroom. In the early years of this library, resources were concentrated mainly upon the reference library and reading room, but facilities for borrowing were provided from 1853 onwards through two branch libraries, accommodated at first in schools (with schoolteachers as librarians) and afterwards in rented houses. This idea of branch libraries was quickly imitated in other large towns.

The other important civic library in this first phase was at Birmingham. Here plans were made from the start for a central library and four branch lending libraries, and service commenced in the Constitution Hill branch in 1861. The specially erected central library, including both reference and lending departments, was opened in 1865–66. The library committee here laid down three principles to govern the selection of books. One was that they should as far as practicable represent every phase of human thought; the second was that they should be chiefly books of permanent value and of standard interest; and the third was that they should include

68. WESTMINSTER'S FIRST PUBLIC LIBRARY, 1857
The library established by the parishes of St Margaret and St John, in the premises of the former Westminster Literary and Scientific Institution. *Westminster City Libraries*

'those rare and costly works which are generally out of the reach of individual students and collectors'.

Other libraries of this period were mainly either in the county towns (including the university towns of Oxford and Cambridge) or in industrial centres such as Sheffield (opened in 1856), Bolton, Birkenhead, Blackburn, Sunderland and Walsall. It was the industrial areas that took the lead in providing a library service, and indeed a map of public library development in the late nineteenth century would closely parallel the development of mechanics' institutes at an earlier date. London at this time, and for more than thirty years after the first Public Libraries Act, had only one rate-aided library, established by the parishes of St Margaret and St John at Westminster in 1857. Wales and Scotland were also backward, with libraries only at Cardiff (1862) and in the Lanarkshire mining town of Airdrie (1853).

The new era of political and social reform ushered in by the 1867 Reform Act provided a more favourable climate for library growth, and the Education Act of 1870 and its successors provided a useful starting point for new efforts in many parts of the country to secure the adoption of the Libraries Act. With the advent of Leeds in 1870 and Bristol in 1876 the list of library authorities included every major city outside London except Edinburgh and Glasgow.

Leeds quickly took its place alongside Manchester, Liverpool and Birmingham as one of the largest public libraries in the country. Accommodation for the central reference and lending library was formed by converting the Old Infirmary, but because Leeds was such a sprawling city it was felt necessary to make more than the usual provision for suburban services. This problem was economically if not very efficiently solved by establishing small collections of books in school premises, and in 1885 one-third of the total lending stock was divided among 25 branch libraries.

An interesting feature of the Bristol situation is that the starting point of the new library service was the old town library, which as we have related above was presented to the city by Robert Redwood in 1615. In the eighteenth century this library, and the building which housed it, had been passed for safe keeping to a private subscription library, but in 1855 the Corporation resumed possession, appointed a city librarian, and began to make an annual grant for book purchase. It was not until more than twenty years later that powers were taken under the Public Libraries Acts to provide a full library service. One factor which contributed to this development was a letter addressed to the city fathers by sixteen working men and published in 1871 under the title *The Cry of the Poor*. The letter was a plea for better civic amenities, including a free library:

We should be glad to be able to sit in our own room and read a bit out of an interesting book to our wives and families, or to get one of the children to read to us. Such a book would keep our boys from idling at street corners, where they learn no end of wicked-ness and mischief, and would, maybe, prevent many of them from going to the public house, the dancing rooms, and to the bad.

By the close of 1886 the total number of authorities operating a library service had risen to 125, embracing nearly one-quarter of the total population. The main concentration continued to be in the industrial areas of England: Lancashire, with 18 libraries operating, had half as many libraries again as Scotland, and three times as many as Wales. London still lagged behind, but a second rate-aided library was opened at Wandsworth in 1885, and the Guildhall Library was made available as a public reference library in 1872. This was a new Guildhall Library, not connected in any way with the fifteenth-century foundation described above. It was established in 1828 as a repository for material relating to the City of London, and developed over the years into a most important and valuable collection.

The patriotic fervour engendered by Queen Victoria's Jubilee in 1887 opened up a still more rapid phase in library development. In the mid-nineties nearly a score of new libraries commenced service each year, and the three years 1905–7 saw the creation of more than a hundred new authorities. There was a sharp falling off after 1909, but this was simply because almost every local authority which could afford to run a library on a penny rate had now got one. By the close of 1918 there were, in spite of some absorptions and amalgamations, 566 library authorities in Great Britain, covering in all more than 60 per cent of the population. There were 423 authorities in England, 61 in Wales, and 82 in Scotland.

Many factors contributed to this remarkable growth. The Jubilee itself was one: others were the new demands of technical education following the Technical Instruction Act of 1889; the simplification of adoption procedure under the Public Libraries Act of 1893; the stimulus arising from the reorganisation of local government; and the steady rise in rate income resulting from population growth and industrial and commercial development. Nothing, however, did so much to encourage recalcitrant authorities to act as the availability of generous grants in aid from private benefactors, above all from the Scottish-American steel magnate, Andrew Carnegie. As Carnegie himself remarked at the opening of the new King's Lynn library in 1905, 'There are few doors which a golden key will not unlock.'

Carnegie's grants were in aid of building costs, and were given on

69. TWO LIBRARY BENEFACTORS
Left Andrew Carnegie. *Right* J. Passmore Edwards. *Newham Libraries*

the condition that the local authority concerned must adopt the Libraries Act and levy the full penny rate. He began with a modest grant of £8000 to his native town of Dunfermline in Scotland, where the Carnegie library was duly opened in 1883. Later he extended his operations to England, and in 1913 he created the Carnegie United Kingdom Trust to carry on his philanthropic activities. By that time he had already spent or promised close on £2 millions in aid of public libraries in the United Kingdom. When he died in 1919 it was reported that more than half the library authorities in Great Britain had received grants in aid, and that in the United Kingdom as a whole 380 library buildings were associated with his name. In Scotland, indeed, it seems safe to say that most of the library authorities established before the First World War owed their existence to the promise or the hope of a Carnegie grant.

Carnegie was, it should be said, only the most distinguished among many library benefactors. From the very beginning the great weak-

70. KEIGHLEY PUBLIC LIBRARY: THE FIRST CARNEGIE LIBRARY IN ENGLAND
Carnegie agreed to make a grant of £10,000 to Keighley in 1899, and the central
library there, in the best Board School style, was opened in 1904.

ness of most libraries was lack of funds, and there were many instances
in which wealthy private individuals came forward to supply the need.
The only one who came anywhere near rivalling Carnegie was John
Passmore Edwards, a Cornishman who made a fortune as a publisher
in London. In his later years he gave most generously in support of
libraries and charitable institutions, his library benefactions during
the years 1890–1905 including fifteen public libraries in and around
London, eight in his native Cornwall, and one in Devon. During the
same period he also presented some 70,000 books to public libraries
and other institutions.

Of lesser benefactors one could make a long list – men such as
Sir William Brown at Liverpool, Michael Thomas Bass at Derby,
Sir William Gilstrap at Newark, Edmund Robert Harris at Preston,
Sir Peter Coats at Paisley, and many others. Their names are now
almost forgotten, but in their own towns and in their own generation
these men often made a vital contribution to library development. One
who is better known was Sir Henry Tate, the sugar manufacturer,
who made substantial gifts towards public libraries in London, and is
remembered as the founder of the Tate Gallery.

The major centres in which a library service was inaugurated

71. THE PASSMORE EDWARDS LIBRARY, HAMMERSMITH
A good example of Victorian Romanesque, designed by Maurice B. Adams and
opened in 1896.

between 1887 and 1918 were Edinburgh (1890), Hull (1893), and
Glasgow (1899). At Hull the citizens four times refused to adopt
the Acts. One of the foremost champions of a library service was
James Reckitt, Quaker, Liberal, teetotaller, and wealthy local
manufacturer. After the fourth failure, in 1888, he decided to set an
example by providing a library service for the eastern part of the
town. From his own pocket he paid for the erection of a lending and
reference library, equipped it with 8000 books, and subscribed the
equivalent of a penny rate (about £500) annually for its maintenance.
Even this generous gesture left many ratepayers unconvinced, but
when the proposal for adoption next came forward, in 1892, it was
carried by a narrow margin. The original Reckitt Library was then
taken over as a branch library for East Hull.

The unwillingness of Edinburgh and Glasgow to establish a
public library service is remarkable, bearing in mind the keen
interest the Scots have usually displayed in educational activities.
Of the other two major cities of Scotland, Dundee had a useful library
begun in 1869 and handsomely housed in the Albert Memorial
Institute; and even Aberdeen, in spite of its reputation for parsimony,
had inaugurated a library service in 1884, in the former mechanics'

72. A VISIT BY CARNEGIE
On his frequent visits to libraries, Carnegie was received almost with the deference due to royalty. He is here seen, in his old age, visiting the Public Library at Airdrie in 1906. This was one of the many Scottish libraries he had helped to build. *Monklands Libraries*

institute. Eight years later, when a new and larger building was needed, it was provided mainly by public subscription, with only a small contribution from Carnegie.

The citizens of Edinburgh and Glasgow, however, were adamant. In Edinburgh, in 1881, sandwichmen paraded the streets calling upon ratepayers to 'Resist this Free Library Dodge'. It cost Carnegie £50,000 to overcome this opposition, but at last in 1890 a splendid new library, regarded at the time as the last word in library architecture, was opened on George IV Bridge. Unfortunately, in the period up to the First World War, the funds available were never adequate to develop a really efficient library service, and branch development in particular was very backward.

Glasgow was more fortunate. Here, between 1876 and 1888, the citizens three times rejected a proposal to adopt the Acts, and they

73. ORIGINAL STAFF OF THE CARNEGIE LIBRARY IN EDINBURGH, 1890
The Librarian, Hew Morrison, is third from the left on the front row. The presence
of two lady assistants is unusual at this period. *Edinburgh City Libraries*

never in fact gave their approval. After 1894 a poll was no longer
necessary, and in 1899 the Corporation dealt with the matter by
including a special clause in a local Act. Unlike Edinburgh, however,
Glasgow already had the makings of a complete central library
service. The old Stirling's Library, bequeathed to the Corporation
in 1791, was now amalgamated with a private subscription library, but
remained open to the public for reference purposes. Another non-
rate-aided reference library, the Mitchell Library, had been founded
in 1877 under a bequest to the Corporation from Stephen Mitchell,
tobacco manufacturer, and with some assistance from public funds
(from the 'whisky money' and other sources) had already built up a
substantial collection. This at once became the city's central reference
library, and when in 1911 it became necessary to move it to a larger
building, Stirling's Library was moved into the former Mitchell

building and became the central lending library. In the meantime the Library Committee had also embarked on the provision of branch libraries. Thanks mainly to the munificence of Carnegie, who gave £115,000 for the building of fourteen branches, they were able by 1915 to create a network of branches covering the whole city. Thus within a few short years Glasgow had acquired a library system which could challenge comparison with any in the country.

It was at this period that London and the Home Counties at last began to come into the library picture. In what is now Inner London, where there had been three library authorities at the time of the Jubilee, there were more than thirty in operation in 1900. The London Government Act which came into operation in that year, reducing the number of local authorities to twenty, brought a further improvement, for most of the new metropolitan boroughs adopted the Libraries Acts and inaugurated a library service within the next few years. The generosity of Carnegie and Passmore Edwards had not a little to do with these developments: it was Carnegie's offer of £40,000 for a central library and four branch libraries which in 1904 finally overcame the stubborn opposition of Islington. Paddington, Bethnal Green and St Marylebone, however, remained proof against all blandishments, and did not in fact adopt the Acts till after the war.

In what is now Outer London, the growth was almost as rapid. The Home Counties were then much more rural than now, but their villages and market towns, especially those with convenient access by rail, were increasingly being taken over by London commuters. A little cluster of library authorities had already sprung up in the early 'eighties on the western fringes of London, in centres such as Wimbledon, Twickenham and Richmond, and soon there were many more, making by the end of the century a ring of libraries round the entire city.

This brief sketch of library development may convey the impression that by 1918 (or indeed by 1914, since very little happened during the First World War) most of the country had already been provided with a library service. In a sense this is true, but the statement can be accepted only with two serious qualifications. In the first place, as we shall see shortly, the quality of library service varied enormously between one authority and another. In the second place, effective development was still restricted mainly to the urban areas, and especially to the industrial areas. In the industrial North and Midlands almost every town had its library, but there were vast tracts of rural England, and still more rural Wales and Scotland, with little or no provision. It is true that there were by the end of the period about a hundred rural parishes which had adopted the Libraries Acts (the first was Tarves, in Aberdeenshire, in 1883) but only about three-quarters of them had done anything to implement the Acts, and many of these were libraries in little more than name. It was estimated in 1913 that 79 per cent of the urban population had access to public library facilities, compared with 2·4 per cent of the rural population.

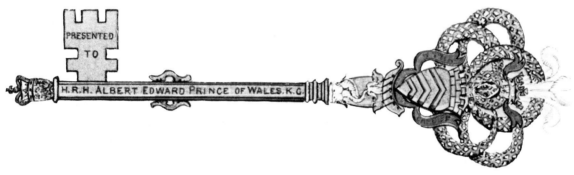

74. A GOLDEN KEY
Design for the key used at the opening of the Cardiff Central Library Extension by Edward Prince of Wales in 1896. *South Glamorgan Libraries*

Further Reading

Two biographies by W. A. Munford provide a detailed narrative of the events leading up to the Public Libraries Act of 1850. They are *William Ewart, M.P.* (Grafton 1960), and *Edward Edwards, 1812–1886* (Library Association 1963). There are good accounts also in John Minto, *A History of the Public Library Movement in Great Britain and Ireland* (Allen and Unwin 1932), and in W. J. Murison, *The Public Library: its Origins, Purpose and Significance* (Harrap 1955, 2nd edn. 1971). For the real flavour of the period, however, the reader should turn to the *Report of the Select Committee on Inquiry into Drunkenness* (Parliamentary Papers 1834); the first *Report of the Select Committee on Public Libraries* (Parliamentary Papers 1849); and the columns of Hansard's *Parliamentary Debates*, 3rd Ser., Vols. 109–111 (1850).

The general development of the library service from 1850 to the First World War can be traced in Edward Edwards, *Free Town Libraries* (1869); in the successive editions of Thomas Greenwood's *Free Public Libraries* (1886, 2nd edn. 1887, 3rd edn., under the title *Public Libraries*, 1890, 4th edn. 1891, 4th edn. revised 1894); and in the year books which Greenwood subsequently launched. *Greenwood's Library Year Book, 1897* (1897), and the *British Library Year Book, 1900–1901* (1900), were both edited by Greenwood himself. They were followed by the *Libraries, Museums and Art Galleries Year Book* (various editors) of which the first two editions were for 1910–11 and 1914 respectively.

Greenwood was very much a committed observer of the library scene. J. J. Ogle, though a librarian, gives a more balanced view in *The Free Library* (1897). For 1913–14 we have a valuable objective report prepared by W. G. S. Adams for the Carnegie Trust, *A Report on Library Provision and Policy* (Carnegie U.K. Trust, Dunfermline 1915).

There is no satisfactory general account of Carnegie's work for public libraries, but the work of Passmore Edwards is commemorated in J. J. Macdonald, *Passmore Edwards Institutions* (1900).

Poverty and Progress 3

Libraries for the Working Class

We have seen that throughout the late nineteenth and early twentieth centuries public libraries were commonly thought of as being chiefly for the working class. They had about them the odour of charity, and their charitable character was often confirmed by the use of the title 'Free Library'. This title, which may still be seen carved in stone over the portals of some old library buildings, was useful in distinguishing public libraries from the proprietary subscription libraries which continued to cater for the well-to-do, especially as many of these had already pre-empted the title 'Public Library'. The word 'Free', however, had unfortunate connotations. Thomas Greenwood's first book on the subject, published in 1886, was called *Free Public Libraries*, but he afterwards recognised that this description was inaccurate and misleading, and from his third edition (1890) 'Free' was dropped from the title.

In point of fact the users of public libraries were by no means drawn exclusively from the working classes. This is a matter on which we have a great deal of information, for libraries at this period commonly kept elaborate records, including very often details of the occupations of their readers. For the years 1876 and 1877 we also have Parliamentary Returns giving occupational statistics for thirty-seven libraries. From these it is clear that public libraries were being extensively used by people from the working and lower middle classes – labourers, artisans, clerks, shop assistants and the like. The lists also included, however, quite appreciable numbers of accountants, architects, clergymen, merchants, manufacturers, medical men, schoolteachers, and other professional and middle-class people – indeed, bearing in mind the numerical predominance of the working class in the population the extent of use by other classes is surprisingly high. Leeds in 1876 claimed that 15 per cent of its reference library users were merchants and professional men, but these figures are

75. NORWICH CITY LIBRARY
The first purpose-built public library in the country, opened in 1857, and de-
molished in 1964. Note the inscription FREE LIBRARY over the entrance.
Norfolk County Library

exceptional and should probably be treated with caution.

Because universal education was still a new phenomenon most
readers and borrowers were very young. In 1876–7, when 14 was still
usually the minimum age for library membership, it was common for
about one-third of users to be under 21, and for the majority of users to
be under 30. The readers under 21 would be mainly schoolboys,
apprentices, and junior employees in offices and shops. The middle-
aged and elderly were therefore much under-represented. So also
were women and girls, who seem to have averaged something like
20 per cent of lending library users, and an even smaller percentage
of reference library users. The higher education of women was still
very ill provided for.

No detailed study has yet been made of library users in the later
nineteenth and early twentieth centuries. In the 'nineties at least

the position does not seem to have changed very much. For the year 1907 we have a calculation made by J. D. Brown from a survey of library annual reports. This produces the following broad groupings for the users of lending libraries: domestic, 7 per cent; professional, 7 per cent; students and scholars, 20 per cent; industrial (trades) 20 per cent; commercial, 29 per cent; unclassified, 17 per cent. In spite of the vagueness of this classification, it is again clear that the users were not exclusively working-class. The emphasis on youth also remained; because of the introduction of children's libraries nearly half the borrowers were under 20, and nearly three-quarters under 40. There was, however, a big change in the position of women and girls, who now, according to Brown, accounted for 41 per cent of the borrowers.

Librarians, of course, were for the sake of their own self-esteem only too anxious to present their libraries as institutions serving all classes of society. Edward Edwards, Manchester's first city librarian, set forth the principle quite uncompromisingly as early as 1859, in his monumental *Memoirs of Libraries*:

> Supported alike by the taxation of the wealthiest capitalist and of the humblest householder, they must be so formed, so augmented, and so governed as to be alike useful to both. They must in no sense be 'professional libraries', or 'tradesmen's libraries', or 'working men's libraries', but 'town libraries'.

James Picton, for many years chairman of the Liverpool Library Committee, supported this view when he declared in 1875: 'It must be remembered that this institution is not for a class or a community. It is the common property of all, irrespective of rank, station or circumstances.' And in 1883 Cambridge's first librarian, John Pink, proudly claimed: 'In the Free Library may be seen sitting side by side the MA and the mechanic, the Undergraduate and the School-boy, men in broadcloth and boys in fustian.'

In spite of these democratic pretensions, however, and in spite of the figures which in some measure supported them, the public image of the libraries remained obstinately working-class, and this is reflected in the poverty and often meanness of the library service provided.

Finance, of course, was the great weakness. The $\frac{1}{2}$d rate granted by the 1850 Act was totally inadequate. The 1d rate which shortly became available was perhaps just sufficient, at the outset, for the larger authorities, but was quite insufficient for the many small authorities which came into existence after the population limit was removed in 1866. Even the larger authorities soon began to find their development constricted, and pressure on resources increased as their libraries grew in size. W. R. Credland, librarian of Manchester, calculated in 1883 that the minimum income required to support a library service was £500 per annum, and that in over forty of the hundred or so libraries then existing the annual income was below this figure. Nineteen libraries had less than £200 a year, and some as little as £40. Tarves in Aberdeenshire, the first rural parish library, which opened in 1884, made do with an income of £20 a year.

The evil was compounded, in the early years, by the niggardliness of authorities which refused to levy the full 1d rate. Oxford, Cambridge, Leicester, Blackburn, Bolton and Sheffield were among the libraries which had to be content, at least at times, with a $\frac{1}{2}$d or $\frac{3}{4}$d rate. In Sheffield, in the years 1875–77, the total amount available for the purchase of books for the central library and three branches was £35 3s 7d. Even where the full 1d rate was levied it sometimes had to support not only a library but also a museum, an art gallery, or science classes. Cardiff, on a $\frac{1}{2}$d rate, supported both a museum and science classes.

Many libraries were driven to appeal for public subscriptions, and not a few resorted to the device of running a subscription lending library for their wealthier users, alongside the free library. This was a practice that persisted, in many cases, into the twentieth century. At Dundee, where it began in 1876, and lasted till 1943, the subscribers paid a guinea a year, and the subscriptions were used to purchase books which were available for the first year to subscribers only, and then passed into the general library. Quite apart from the class distinction involved, a great drawback of such an arrangement was, as one experienced librarian commented, that it led to the acquisition by the library of a mass of ephemeral literature, especially fiction. To hard-pressed libraries, however, it was better to have the shelves filled with ephemeral literature than not to have them filled at all. Some libraries augmented their scanty supply by a subscription to Mudie's or W. H. Smith's.

Towards the end of the century the position improved somewhat. This was partly because the Technical Instruction Act of 1889 and the Museums Act of 1891 made separate funds available for technical classes and museums, and partly because many library authorities secured special legislation empowering them to raise more than a 1d rate. By 1914 more than fifty places had done this, including most of the leading provincial towns. The position of the smaller authorities, however, remained desperate. In 1910–11 there were still 55 libraries in England, and 44 in Wales and Scotland, with incomes less than £100 per annum, and well over half had incomes under £500 per annum. It was fortunate that these years brought no great increase in prices. The index of commodity prices was almost the same in 1910

CARDIFF LIBRARIAN: "Oh dear, Mr. Corporation, I do wish you would remove this barrier; it is very inconvenient and doesn't allow me room to do my work properly."

76. THE BARRIER OF THE PENNY RATE
The City Librarian of Cardiff struggles in vain to meet the demand for books from all parts of the city: a cartoon in the local *Evening Express*, 1897. By this time the library had the full penny rate, but it was still inadequate. The Librarian, John Ballinger (*inset*) left in 1908 to become first librarian of the National Library of Wales, and was later knighted. *South Glamorgan Libraries*

as in 1850, and the retail price of books fell significantly. From the 'eighties onwards new novels, which had hitherto normally been published in three volumes at 10s 6d a volume, began to be published in single-volume form at 5s or 6s, while reprints of standard fiction and non-fiction, formerly 3s 6d or 5s, might now be had in a reasonable cloth binding for as little as a shilling. By the early years of the twentieth century this was the price of several reputable series, for example Nelson's Classics, which began in 1900, the World's Classics, which began in 1901, and Dent's Everyman Library, which began in 1906.

Even so most libraries were very small, and were giving a very indifferent service. Nearly nine-tenths of all libraries in 1913–14 possessed fewer than 50,000 volumes, and more than half the total had fewer than 10,000 volumes – about half the number which would nowadays be considered appropriate for a modest branch library. Some were small because, as at Canterbury and Winchester, the main focus of interest was the museum, to which the library was merely an appendage. Canterbury in 1870 (twenty-three years after the opening) had a total stock of about 2600 books, 'some very old'. They were little used either for reference or for lending, loans averaging about 14 per week. In general, however, these libraries were in small towns and villages which just had not the resources to provide an adequate service. A lending library and reading room was all that most could manage, and some had even less. 'Collection of books in Reading Room' was the description applied in 1913–14 to the library of Letcombe Regis, a small village in Berkshire with a total library income of £6 a year. It is a description which could have been applied to many libraries in larger centres. Cratfield, in Suffolk, had 200 volumes kept in the Parish Council Offices, issues being about one a week. Great Wyrley, in Staffordshire, had 500 volumes available through three delivery stations. Such libraries were seldom open for more than a few hours a day, and had to rely on honorary or part-time librarians.

In between the great libraries and these very small ones came the general run of libraries serving the medium-sized market and industrial towns. It is in these libraries that the working-class aspect of the service can be most clearly seen.

Library Buildings

Accommodation was always the first problem. A few places, as we have seen, were fortunate enough to find private benefactors to present them with buildings. Fewer still, like Norwich, found the money to build for themselves. For the most part, however, public libraries had to make do with other people's leavings: disused town halls and council offices, redundant schools, hospitals and gaols. Leeds made a start in the Old Infirmary, Northampton in the County Gaol, Stockport in a room over the market hall, where the odour of books and readers mingled with the smell of cheese from the stalls below. Quite often an arrangement was made to take over the building (and perhaps the stock) of a decaying mechanics' institute, athenaeum,

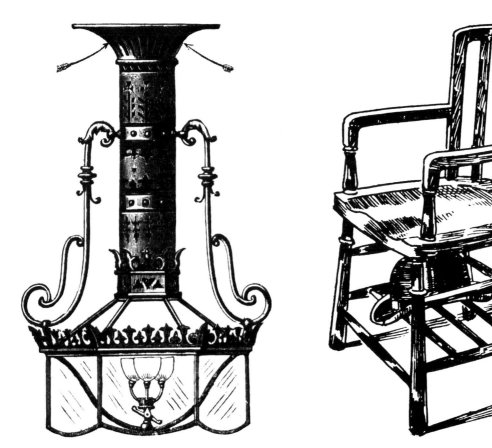

77. LIBRARY EQUIPMENT
Left Sugg's Patent Ventilating 'Taj' Light: gas jets protected by glass and provided with a chimney for ventilation. Advertised in Greenwood's *Public Libraries*, 1894. *Right* Combined chair, hat-rack and umbrella-stand for the reading room, pictured in J. D. Brown's *Manual of Library Economy*, 1903.

literary institute, or private subscription library; and in default of all else resort might be had to rented rooms.

These makeshift premises were nearly always in some way unsuitable. They were commonly overcrowded, and they might also be ill-lighted, ill-heated, ill-ventilated, and generally inconvenient. By the end of the nineteenth century most libraries were heated by low pressure hot water systems, which were clumsy but reasonably efficient, but many smaller libraries still relied on coal fires, which warmed the few at the expense of the many. Electric lighting was beginning to be used at this time – Liverpool was the first to introduce it in 1881 – but was still too expensive for most libraries. The usual alternative was gas lighting, initially by means of gas jets, which gave a very poor light indeed, especially if, as was often the case, they were placed high up, well away from the books and reader. The introduction of the incandescent gas mantle in the 'eighties was a great improvement, but gas lighting was still a worry to librarians, not only because of the fire risk, but also because the heat and fumes were believed to be injurious to the books, and were certainly disagreeable to the staff, especially where, as was often the case, the bookshelves reached up to ceiling height.

At a conference of the recently formed Library Association at Cambridge in 1882, Peter Cowell, city librarian of Liverpool, described to his envious fellow delegates the introduction of electric lighting in the central library at Liverpool. For the staff it had brought 'a wonderful freedom from that feeling of weariness and lassitude which invariably more or less oppresses us when working by gas'. Some readers, however, had complained that the new light was too brilliant, and one had alleged that it gave him neuralgia. The light was provided at this time, incidentally, by arc lamps: the now familiar incandescent electric lamp had only just been invented.

The generosity of Carnegie and other large-scale benefactors brought, of course, a great improvement in library buildings. More and more authorities, old and new, were now able to acquire purpose-built premises, carefully planned to provide, within the limits of the money available, the best and most efficient accommodation possible. Much attention now began to be paid to the design of library buildings, and new libraries received considerable attention in the professional journals. In 1911 the Carnegie Corporation, from its long experience in this field, produced a leaflet called *Notes on the Erection of Library Buildings*, which had a great influence on the design of branches and other small libraries. The Corporation recommended a simple rectangular plan, on a single floor, divided as necessary by moveable bookstacks. This simple functional design gave maximum flexibility and ease of supervision.

A new building, however, was not always an unmixed blessing. The Carnegie benefactions were, indeed, yet another example of a delusion which bedevilled library history for more than half a century – the delusion that if only a building can be provided a library service is automatically guaranteed. Many small authorities now found themselves, to their consternation, the possessors of splendid buildings whose upkeep absorbed so much of their limited rateable income that they had little or nothing left to spend on books or staff. Professor W. G. S. Adams of Oxford, who was invited by the Carnegie Trustees, on the eve of the First World War, to prepare a report on *Library Provision and Policy*, identified the problem clearly, citing among many other examples of overbuilding one library with a £10,000 Carnegie building which in the year 1914 could afford only £1 for books. The authority concerned is not identified, but may have been Dumfries, of which it is recorded that when the library was completed in 1903, 'in all its columned splendour,' there was 'not a single book on the shelves nor a single penny in the bank with which to buy one'. It was necessary to borrow money to provide the initial stock.

The Adams Report provides information about many aspects of library organisation, and among other things about the development of branch libraries. The largest libraries, faced with rapidly expanding populations, were by this date engaged in their second or even third round of branch provision, but many smaller authorities were just beginning to make such provision for the first time, and many more were either too small to need branches or too poor to provide them. The 533 library authorities listed by Adams had a total of 345 branches and 33 branch reading rooms, but eight large libraries accounted for one-third of all the branches, and there were more than 400 authorities with no branches at all.

Reading Rooms and their Users

The basic library departments at this time were the reading room, the lending library, and the reference library, in that order, but branches did not always offer a complete service. Some had reading room and lending library only, some no more than a reading room. Many were part-time, open only in the evenings or on certain days of the week. Some authorities, as a substitute for branches, created 'delivery stations', usually in shops, where the shopkeeper undertook in return for a small honorarium to receive lists of wants from enrolled borrowers, and to issue the books when they were sent by the central library. Bradford had travelling library centres in outlying villages, to which boxes of books were sent from time to time.

The important role of the reading room derived from the fact that working people tended to do much of their reading in the library itself. Dingy as it might be, the library offered comforts which all too often they could not expect to find in their own homes – light, warmth and quietness. Larger libraries would often have several reading rooms – a general reading room, a newspaper room, a ladies' reading room, sometimes also a youths' or young people's reading room.

The provision of newspapers was from the beginning the subject of considerable controversy. A clause making such provision possible was included in the Public Libraries Act of 1855, being justified by Sir Alexander Cockburn, Attorney General, on the ground that 'if they shut out newspapers from libraries, they would deprive them of one of the principal attractions to be found in public libraries'. Liverpool was at first exceptional in refusing to provide newspapers,

78. AN EARLY NEWSPAPER ROOM
Cotton operatives in Manchester reading the latest news from America during the Civil War, from the *Illustrated London News*, 1862. *Radio Times Hulton Picture Library*

but from 1883 onwards made liberal provision not only in its central library but in five evening reading rooms in schools. This policy evidently led to some criticism, and the library committee in its thirty-eighth annual report (1891) felt impelled to comment on the view that lending libraries and reading rooms should not provide works of fiction, periodicals, and newspapers. The demand for such literature, they argued, was the natural outcome of the decision to establish a national system of elementary education. This committed the country to the supply of 'adequate means by which the people can make use of their intellectual faculties, and can continue the education thus begun in the school, or make use of it for the purpose of recreation'. The report continued:

Thus Public Libraries, Museums, and Art Galleries have ceased to be merely the resorts of the cultured, but have become the gathering places of the people. They are no longer merely

79. READING ROOM AT THE CANTON BRANCH, CARDIFF
A photograph dating from the early years of the present century. *South Glamorgan Libraries*

the repositories of books of standard authors and articles of *vertu* and high art; they must also satisfy our new social conditions and minister to the intellectual entertainment of the masses. Viewed in this light the demand for works of fiction, magazines, and newspapers is not surprising, and it is one which ought to and must be met, for while this light literature satisfies the craving of the intellect for occupation, it is in itself a valuable means of education, and one which, no doubt, often serves as a stimulus and incentive to reading of a more serious character.

There were frequent complaints that reading rooms, and especially newspaper rooms, were the haunt of tramps and other undesirables who came in merely for warmth and shelter. It is true that many people, including tramps, came into libraries to keep warm. Some came merely to read the betting odds, and in the 'nineties not a few libraries adopted the practice of blacking out the betting news. At times of unemployment the newspaper rooms were crowded out

with working people struggling to look at the 'Situations Vacant' pages, and some libraries, to ease the congestion, posted these pages up on notice-boards outside the building.

By the close of the nineteenth century many librarians were beginning to have serious doubts about the value of newspaper provision. It was pointed out that whereas when public libraries began in the early 1850s a newspaper usually cost 5d and was beyond the reach of the working man, now thanks to the enterprise of publishers and the abolition of newspaper taxes a wide range of papers was available at 1d or even ½d (the ½d *Daily Mail* was launched by the Harmsworth brothers in 1896). There were also objections on other grounds. E. A. Savage, librarian of Coventry and afterwards of Edinburgh, describes in his usual vivid and racy style how in his younger days 'all the verminous old soaks, in the days of cheap potent booze, sang in the pubs and streets and police cells when they had money, and when it was gone, crept to the newsrooms whence they had to be carried out with the tongs'. James Duff Brown, whose *Manual of Library Economy*, first published in 1903, became the standard work on library administration, expressed the view that 'the habitual newspaper reader is a man who rarely reads anything else', and when he became librarian of Islington in 1905 he persuaded his committee to dispense with a newsroom. Most librarians at this period, however, were less courageous, or less influential: they recognised the nuisance and dealt with it as best they could.

It was to protect women and girls from possible unpleasantness that the early libraries provided, whenever they could afford it, separate ladies' reading rooms, and these long continued in use in some places – at Stamford in Lincolnshire as late as the 1960s. The necessity for them, however, was already being called into question in 1890, when Thomas Greenwood commented that 'a separate ladies' room means very often a good deal of gossip, and sometimes it is from these rooms that fashion-sheets and plates from the monthlies are most missed'. J. D. Brown in 1907 counted about eighty libraries still making separate provision for ladies, and thought it was nonsense to suppose that women are 'delicate creatures requiring seclusion in glass cases'.

Adolescents formed such a large proportion of library readers at this period, and were so liable to be a nuisance to their elders, that some libraries made a separate youths' reading room, the earliest example of this being at Westminster, where the library of St Margaret and St John opened in 1857. From Manchester, where boys' reading rooms were introduced in 1878, we have a vivid description written by the librarian, W. R. Credland, in 1895:

80. LADIES' READING ROOM, GLASGOW
The Ladies' Reading Room at the Woodside Branch, from a *Descriptive Handbook*
of 1907. *Glasgow City Libraries*

The rooms are each provided with about five hundred volumes, carefully chosen for their suitability to the class of boys who are likely to use them, and a selection of equally suitable periodicals is also supplied. It is quite true to say that during the winter months they are, throughout the whole evening, crowded with lads busily engaged in assimilating the literature provided for them. There can hardly be a more pleasing and suggestive sight than is presented by any one of these rooms, with its bright lighting, its busy and helpful female attendants, and its crowd of readers eager for amusement or instruction. And the boys themselves are of that age and class which it is most desirable to influence for good. They are for the most part children of parents whose poverty draws them perilously near to the borderland of crime, but they are still too young to have crossed that border themselves. It is just such lads as these whom it is essential to detach from vicious companions, and to surround with every possible influence that can tend to moral and social improvement,

81. BOOK-REACHER
Preserved at the
Norwich City
Library. *Norfolk
County Library*

if they are to be made into useful men and good citizens, and rescued from absorption into the pauper and criminal classes.

The persistence of the moral improvement motive in library work comes out very clearly in this passage.

Provision for adolescents eventually led on to provision for children. Most of the early libraries had a lower age limit, usually 14, but a few, notably Birmingham from its commencement in 1861, catered for younger children, and eventually this became, as it is today, an important part of library work.

Books behind Bars

In view of the origins of public libraries, one would have expected that libraries and library committees would take special pains to welcome working-class readers and make them feel at home, but this was by no means universally so. Liverpool, when its library opened in 1852, did indeed decree 'that all persons, however ragged or poor, shall be treated as gentlemen,' and the first librarian, J. S. Dalton, believed that this contributed to the good order and decorum which was maintained in the reading room. Some other libraries sought to create something of the social atmosphere which characterised the mechanics' institutes: facilities were made available for games such as chess and draughts, and in some cases a smoking room was provided. All too often, however, the attitude was one of suspicion.

Some libraries which opened in the 'fifties and 'sixties, Manchester and Norwich, for example, were so nervous about admitting the working classes that at their opening they actually called in the help of the police to prevent disorder. Such extreme measures were soon proved unnecessary, but even in later years the library reader was commonly faced with a positive battery of prohibitory notices: SILENCE, NO SPITTING, NO BETTING, NO DOGS, NO BICYCLES, and so forth. J. D. Brown, who was not given to undue exaggeration, commented in 1903 that some of the rules seemed designed to protect the property of the library committee 'from the onslaughts and unwelcome attentions of a horde of goths and vandals'.

It was of a piece with this restrictive attitude that in the lending library, which along with the reading room was the most popular department, it was a cardinal principle that the reader should on no account have access to the shelves to choose his own books. This, it was believed, would certainly lead to theft, disorder, and all kinds of irregularities. Instead, the books were stored behind a counter, commonly in lofty bookstacks of which the upper shelves could be reached only by climbing a tall ladder, or alternatively, by a long-

SHEFFIELD
FREE·PUBLIC·LIBRARIES.

CATALOGUE

OF THE

CENTRAL LIBRARY
LENDING DEPARTMENT.

ADMINISTRATIVE DEPARTMENT.
REFERENCE LIBRARY,
SHEFFIELD

ESTABLISHED 1855

Sheffield:
J. ROBERTSHAW, PRINTER, ST. PETER'S CLOSE, HARTSHEAD.
1882.

PRICE ONE SHILLING.

CATALOGUE.

PART I.

ALPHABETICAL INDEX OF AUTHORS' NAMES.

ABBOTT, C. C. Primitive Industry: Illustrations of the Handiwork in Stone, Bone, and Clay of the Native Races of the Northern Atlantic Seaboard of America 1881 F 349
Abbott, E. A. A Shakespearian Grammar 1869 H 4299
Abbott, E. A. and Seeley, J. R. English Lessons for English People 1871 H 4151
Abbott, Jacob. Franconia Stories H 3845
— Life of Alexander the Great I 379 I 1161
— Life of Alfred the Great I 381
— Life of Charles I. I 380 I 1162
— Life of Charles II. I 382
— Life of Cleopatra, Queen of Egypt I 383 I 1163
— Life of Cyrus the Great I 384 I 1164
— Life of Darius, King of Persia I 385 I 1165
— Life of Elizabeth, Queen of England.. I 386 I 1166
— Life of Hannibal I 387 I 1167
— Life of Julius Cæsar I 389 I 1168 I 1169
— Life of Madame Roland I 394 I 1182
— Life of Marie Antoinette I 390 I 1181
— Life of Mary, Queen of Scots I 391 I 1170
— Life of Nero I 392
— Life of Peter the Great I 499 I 1171
— Life of Pyrrhus I 393 I 1172
— Life of Richard I. I 508
— Life of Richard II. I 769 I 1173
— Life of Richard III. I 770 I 1174
— Life of Romulus I 395 I 1175 I 1176
— Life of the Empress Josephine I 388 I 1180
— Life of William the Conqueror I 396 I 1177 I 1178
— Life of Xerxes I 397
— The Young Christian I 250
Abbott, Rev. J. Editor. Philip Musgrave: Memoirs of a Church of England Missionary in the North American Colonies H 1058
Abbott, John S. C. Heroines of the French Revolution 1858 I 473
— Life of Henry IV., King of France and Navarre I 506 I 1179
Abbott, T. K. Sight and Touch: an attempt to disprove the received (or Berkeleian) Theory of Vision 1864 F 2271 F 2776
A'Beckett, Gilbert A. Comic History of England G 1013 G 4496
— Comic History of Rome G 2464
— The Comic Blackstone 1857 H 2703
Abeken, B. R. Life and Writings of Cicero 1854 G 1641
Abel, C. D. Elementary Principles of Machinery 1868 H 4072

Abercrombie, John, M.D. Elements of Sacred Truth 1844 I 287
— Enquiries concerning the Intellectual Powers 1854 H 810
— Essays and Tracts 1847 H 824
— Harmony of Christian Faith and Character 1845 I 269
— Philosophy of the Moral Feelings 1855 H 811
Abercrombie, J. The Gardener's Pocket Journal 1813 I 298
Aberdeen, Earl of. Principles of Grecian Architecture 1860 H 1829
Abernethy, John, F.R.S. Surgical and Physiological Works 1830 F 1076
— Surgical Observations on the Treatment of Local Diseases 1829 G 1923
Ablett, W. H. English Trees and Tree Planting 1880 F 1081
Abney, W. de W. Instructions in Photography 1876 H 4818
— Treatise on Photography 1878 H 4817
About, E. The Roman Question 1859 G 1208
Accum, F. Culinary Chemistry; or, Scientific Principles of Cookery 1821 G 2148
— Manual of Analytical Mineralogy H 2414
— Treatise on Adulteration of Food, and Culinary Poisons 1820 G 1924
— Treatise on Making Good and Wholesome Bread 1821 G 2147
Achilli, Rev. G. Dealings with the Inquisition 1851 G 2196
Acland, Rev. C. Manners and Customs of India 1857 H 1059
Acland, H. W., and Ruskin, J. The Oxford Museum 1859 H 1758
Acton, E. English Bread Book 1857 H 1634
Adair, R. Sketch of the Character of the late Duke of Devonshire 1811 F 2196
Adam, W. Gem of the Peak G 788 H 203
Adams, Andrew L. Field and Forest Rambles, with Notes, &c., on the Natural History of Eastern Canada 1873 G 444
— Notes of a Naturalist in the Nile Valley and Malta 1870 G 3411
Adams, Arthur. Travels of a Naturalist in Japan and Manchuria 1870 F 2072
Adams, C. See Novels.
Adams, E. Elements of the English Language 1870 G 3476

82. SHEFFIELD CENTRAL LENDING LIBRARY CATALOGUE, 1882
It was with the help of a catalogue such as this that the borrower had to identify the books he needed. The illustration shows the title-page, and the opening page of the Author Index: there was also a Subject Index, which was Part II.
Sheffield Libraries

handled instrument known as a 'book-reacher', which was similar to the apparatus sometimes used for gathering fruit. The reader thumbed through a grubby printed catalogue and passed the number of the book he wanted to the library assistant. Very often it was not in, and another number had to be asked for, perhaps several more numbers, so that on a busy evening the poor assistant was exhausted with scurrying round bookstacks and up and down ladders.

A refinement of this system, which became very popular from the 'eighties onwards, was the use of the 'indicator' – a large board erected at the edge of the lending counter and indicating by numbers which books were in and which out. This saved the time of both reader and assistant. There were many different varieties of indicators, the most popular being the Cotgreave Indicator, designed in 1877 by Alfred Cotgreave, librarian of Wednesbury. A man of restless and inventive turn of mind, Cotgreave was librarian successively of five

83. BRANCH LENDING LIBRARY AT ANDERSTON, GLASGOW, 1907
Note that the borrowers are all young: three young men consult the catalogue, while two young women wait at the counter. Note also the row of indicators. These were not Cotgreave indicators, but they worked on a very similar principle, with a slot for each book. 'Numbers underlined White are in', is the slogan printed over the top. *Glasgow City Libraries*

libraries, ending his career as first librarian of West Ham. He devised a great variety of useful library gadgets, including the 'book-reacher' just referred to, and he also compiled, with immense labour, a *Contents Subject-Index to General and Periodical Literature*, which was published in 1900, and was a valuable pioneering reference tool.

The Cotgreave Indicator was a wooden frame fitted with rows of small slots, one for each book. Each slot held a shallow metal tray with the number of the book marked at each end, usually in blue at one end and red at the other; and each tray held a miniature ledger, one inch wide and three inches long. When a book was in, the blue end of the tray faced towards the reader; when the book was taken out, the tray was removed from the back of the frame, the loan entered in the ledger, and the tray replaced with the red end towards the reader. 'Blue in, red out' was the slogan.

In large libraries, however, the indicator was useless because of the amount of space it occupied. Even for a modest collection of 24,000 volumes Darlington in 1885 had to provide 55 feet of indicators. It was, therefore, mainly in the medium-sized libraries that indicators were used, and even here they were often used for fiction only. At its best, the system was a very poor substitute for direct access to the shelves. E. A. Savage, recalling his early days at the Croydon Central Lending Library, vividly describes the struggle of the assistants to enter the reader's number and the issue date in the fiddling little indicator registers, and the 'crowd of lurching over-heated readers lusting for books,' jammed in front of the indicators.

Few libraries, outside the big cities, were able in their early years to offer their readers a balanced and carefully selected choice of books. Wigan, which in addition to £12,000 for a building received a similar endowment for books, was one of the lucky ones, and prior to the opening in 1878 a team of specialists was recruited to select the books in various subjects, 'great care being taken to include only works of high merit'. Most libraries of comparable size, however, had to build up their stock in a variety of ways. Direct purchase often

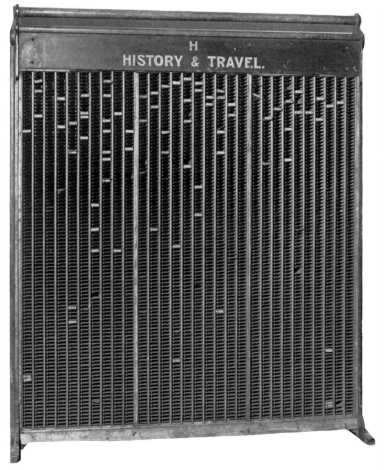

84. A COTGREAVE INDICATOR
Close-up (*left*) of a section of a Cotgreave indicator still surviving at the Norwich City Library. A few of the slots still have their numbered trays, each with its miniature ledger (*right*) in which the library assistant entered the number of the borrower's card and the date of issue. *Norfolk County Library*

accounted for less than half the total, the rest being made up by donations and by books taken over from defunct subscription libraries, mechanics' institutes and similar bodies. A few authorities, e.g. Norwich, Bristol and Newcastle upon Tyne, were able to take over ancient town or parish libraries.

Such sources of supply were very unsatisfactory. Donations were all too often, as Edward Edwards remarked, 'the mere weedings of private collections,' and the stocks acquired from other libraries were seldom in good condition. As to the old town and parish libraries, though they sometimes included works of great rarity, such as the Nantwich Wynkyn de Worde, they consisted in the main of seventeenth- and eighteenth-century divinity. Lending library stocks, because of heavy use and lack of funds for replacements, quickly became worn and dirty, and much of the time of library staff was spent pasting and patching books that should long ago have been relegated to the dustbin.

Then, as now, the main demand of library readers was for fiction, with history, biography and travel next in order of popularity. Throughout the nineteenth century fiction accounted for about one-quarter of lending library stocks, and for about two-thirds of the issues — sometimes for more than four-fifths of the issues. This was a great disappointment to the moralists and to the educational lobby, and provided plenty of ammunition for those who sought to oppose the further spread of the library movement. As late as 1897 Passmore Edwards was accused of 'going about offering public libraries to be upheld at the expense of the ratepayers for lazy fiction-reading people'.

Librarians and library committees were by no means easy in mind about this situation. Some comforted themselves with the question-begging argument that it was the duty of a public library to meet all proper public demands; others struggled, against all the evidence, to maintain the belief that the reading of fiction would lead on to the reading of more solid literature. Controversy raged long and often furiously, and it was only very tardily that people were brought to accept the view that public libraries had a recreational as well as an educative function.

But of course a great deal of serious reading also went on, encouraged from the 'nineties onwards by the practice of providing readers with an additional ticket for non-fiction. For the self-educated working man, the student, the teacher, the businessman, the professional man, the public library was a real godsend, providing books both for educational purposes and for the needs of daily life. In the reference libraries, where the supply of fiction was minimal, the subjects showing the highest percentage of issues, according to statistics published by J. D. Brown in 1907, were history and biography (34 per cent) and science and arts (20 per cent).

In 1897, according to a survey published by J. J. Ogle, librarian of Bootle, the most popular fiction writers were Mrs Henry Wood and Marie Corelli, with Dickens and Mary Elizabeth Braddon (author of *Lady Audley's Secret* and seventy-four other works) bracketed third. The most popular non-fiction writers were Carlyle and Ruskin, others much in demand including J. A. Froude, J. R. Green, T. B. Macaulay, and Shakespeare. This survey, however, did not include the largest libraries.

Libraries as Educational Agencies

In many libraries the educational aspect of the work was emphasised by extension activities of various kinds. Lectures were common everywhere, and continued to flourish until rising prices during the First World War compelled libraries to cut out all inessential expenditure. Liverpool was particularly active in this field. The original local Act under which the library was established empowered the Corporation to organise free scientific lectures, and from 1864–5 until after the Second World War provision continued without a break.

The evolution of the Liverpool programme is interesting. Like the mechanics' institutes before it, the library began by offering substantial courses mainly on scientific subjects – ten or twelve lectures on Natural History, or Chemistry, or Geology, or Art. After a good initial response, however, attendance soon fell away, and the systematic instruction first intended gave way to a miscellany of short courses and single lectures on a variety of topics – science, literature, music, history, antiquities, dramatic readings and so on. The 'oxy-hydrogen lantern' gave an extra boost to the popularity of these events, and the tendency to superficiality was in part countered, from 1878 onwards, by the introduction of twelve-lecture University Extension courses in collaboration with the University of Cambridge.

Extension work under the auspices of Cambridge had begun in 1873, and was quickly taken up by London, Oxford, and the various provincial universities. The demand came in the first instance mainly from women, for whom at this time the facilities available for higher education were exceedingly scanty. It was indeed, a body known as the North of England Association for Promoting the Higher Education of Women which in 1867 took the initiative in arranging a number of pioneer university courses. Working men were also interested, and cooperative societies and mechanics' institutes were amongst the bodies which petitioned Cambridge to give the work its

Opposite
85. GILCHRIST LECTURES
Sketches at the Gilchrist Lectures at the Mossley Mechanics' Institute, Lancashire, 1890. Lectures of this type were often arranged in association with public libraries. As may be seen from the upper picture, there was a large attendance, with the Mayor presiding. Note the 'magic lantern', beginning to be widely used at this time. The lecturer, Dr. Andrew Wilson, in full evening dress, is seen below on the right, and an earnest listener on the left. *Illustrated London News*

official blessing. Because of the high cost of courses, however, and because no support was available from public funds, the audiences for Extension courses were mainly middle-class, and mainly women.

This new form of adult education, which made courses by university scholars available in all parts of the country, was warmly welcomed by public libraries, many of which collaborated in the course arrangements, provided accommodation, and assisted in the provision of books. Libraries also assisted, at this time, in short courses organised by the Gilchrist Trust – an educational trust which from 1878 onwards was active in promoting short courses of popular lectures, usually on science. The popularity which attended some of these events is attested by the fact that for a course of six lectures on 'Other Worlds than Ours', organised by the Bethnal Green library, the Great Assembly Hall in the Mile End Road, which seats 5000 people, was 'packed from floor to roof with an appreciative audience of working people'. Such attendances as this were of course exceptional, but Liverpool in 1903 claimed an average attendance of 700 at nearly 2000 lectures over a 37-year period.

A number of libraries, for example Bootle, Cardiff, and Wolverhampton, developed large programmes of technical classes, drawing grant for the purpose from the Science and Art Department. At Wolverhampton, where the work began in 1873, the range of subjects included mathematics, science, art, English language and literature, French, German, Italian, Spanish and shorthand. At Watford the library, opened in 1874, became the home of all kinds of educational activities, including a School of Art, a School of Music, evening classes in art and science, evening lectures, and a day school. In 1885 it took the grandiose title, 'Watford Public Library and College of Science, Art, Music and Literature'. This association between the library and technical education lasted at Watford till 1919, but elsewhere the responsibility for educational work of this kind was commonly taken over, after 1889, by the new Technical Instruction Committees. At Bootle, when the work was divided in 1900, the librarian J. J. Ogle became head of the Technical School.

Extension activity took many other forms – readings, story half-hours, talks about books, exhibitions, concerts. Study circles were often arranged in association with a body known as the National

Home Reading Union. This now almost forgotten organisation was founded in 1889 on the initiative of Dr John Brown Paton, Principal of the Congregational Institute at Nottingham and a leading figure in many educational movements at this time. It was aimed especially at the needs of the new generation of literate young people emerging as a result of the 1870 Education Act, and its main activity consisted in the publication of courses of guided reading at various levels: Young People's Courses, General Courses, and Special Courses. It also issued booklists, encouraged the formation of reading and discussion circles among those taking the courses, and offered tutorial help to individual readers. All this was, of course, very much in line with public library ideals. In practice the emphasis, after the first few years, came to be mainly on work with young people, and by 1914 70,000 of the 76,000 enrolled members were schoolchildren. In the inter-war years the work of the Union gradually faded out, and publication of the reading courses ceased in 1930.

86. THE LIBRARIAN
A lithograph by E. C. Mountford of J. D. Mullins, Chief Librarian of Birmingham 1865–98, one of the leading English librarians of the nineteenth century. He was a fine scholar and a meticulous administrator – his Daily Routine Book for the reference library listed more than a hundred items to be checked by the staff every day. *Birmingham City Libraries*

There were some librarians, then as now, who objected to extension activities of this kind. J. D. Brown, for example, in 1903, complained about 'the craze for magic-lantern entertainments, lecturettes, reading-circles and so forth,' and argued that libraries must be run for the benefit of the whole community, and not for 'such select portions of it as entomological clubs, photographic societies, school children, teachers, or debating societies'. Most librarians, however, were only too anxious to assist any organisation which seemed likely to stimulate serious reading.

Library Staff

So far we have referred only incidentally to library staff, but in view of the poverty-stricken condition of many public libraries their lot cannot have been an enviable one. This was particularly true in the earlier years, when the usual salary for the librarian of a small or medium-sized library was £50 or £60 a year – rather less than the salary of an uncertificated male assistant teacher in an elementary school. In a small library the librarian often had no assistance, and sometimes had to act as caretaker as well: at best he would have the help of a boy at about 5s a week. The hours of work were long (often twelve hours a day or more), and the working conditions were apt to be unhealthy. There was no training for the post, and it carried no professional status: the librarian was there simply to carry out the instructions of his committee.

Librarians were, in fact, a down-trodden race, shockingly over-worked and underpaid. Most of them, we may be sure, performed their duties conscientiously, if only because they dared not do otherwise, but we cannot help wondering whether some of the caretaker-librarians did not occasionally become impatient, like the caretaker-librarian at the Candleford Mechanics' Institute in the 1880s, of whom Flora Thompson wrote in *Lark Rise to Candleford* that he 'seemed to bear a positive grudge against frequent borrowers'.

> 'Carn't y' make up y'r mind?' he would growl at some lingerer at the shelves. 'Te-ak th' first one y' comes to. It won't be no fuller o' lies than tothers,' and if that admonition failed, he would bring his broom and sweep close round the borrower's feet, not sparing toes or heels.

Conditions improved greatly over the years, and by 1911 the librarian of a medium-sized authority could reckon on earning between £200 and £300 a year, which was more than the salary of a certificated elementary school headmaster. Librarians in some larger libraries were able to earn up to £700 a year, which compares

87. STAFF OF YORK CITY LIBRARY, 1895
An unusually informal group. The library opened in
1893, and the first librarian, seen here third from
left, was Arthur H. Furnish, formerly secretary
of the York Mechanics' Institute, who served until
1929. *North Yorkshire County Library*

88. ONE OF BRITAIN'S FIRST WOMEN CHIEF
LIBRARIANS
Miss Kate Lewtas, Librarian of Blackpool 1891–
1902. Two earlier examples of women chief librarians
are recorded – Mrs H. Eteson, also of Blackpool, and
Mrs Elliot, librarian of Hawick, but photographs of
these two ladies have not survived.

very favourably with the £200 received by Edward Edwards as first
librarian of Manchester. Conditions in some small libraries, however,
remained very unsatisfactory. The *Library Year Book* for 1900–1
shows the librarian at Brechin, in Angus, earning £52 a year for a
66-hour week; while the librarian at Hertford, for a 40-hour week,
received £50 a year and had to pay his own assistant. In 1908 the
recently opened library of Bolton upon Dearne in the West Riding
invited applications for the combined post of 'Caretaker for the
Council Offices and Carnegie Library, and Librarian', at thirty
shillings a week with a free house.

In the larger libraries, too, though the chief librarian had improved
his position, the status and salary of library assistants remained low,
with sub-librarians in 1911 averaging about £100 a year, branch
librarians about £90, and assistant librarians about £50. Fortunately
hours of work had now been reduced to an average of about 45 a week,
and an increasing number of libraries were allowing their assistants
the great privilege of a weekly half-holiday.

In 1871, to overcome a shortage of suitable young men, Manchester began to employ women assistants. The experiment was a success: the young women were punctual, attentive, courteous, contented and cheap. By 1879 there were thirty-one of them at 10s to 18s a week. Other authorities were reluctant to adopt such a startling innovation, and as late as 1910 three-quarters of libraries were still staffed exclusively by males. It was the First World War, which did so much for the liberation of women, which opened the way for librarianship to become predominantly a women's profession.

Some New Developments

So far this account has concerned itself mainly with the smaller and medium-sized libraries. This is right and proper, since as we have seen nine-tenths of public libraries fall into this category. We must not, however, forget the larger libraries, many of which, having by local legislation escaped from the limitations of the penny rate, were by 1914 well equipped and giving very good service. The five giants were Glasgow, Birmingham, Manchester, Liverpool and Leeds. All these had now built up substantial bookstocks: Glasgow (though the most recent of the five) was already approaching the half-million mark; Birmingham and Manchester had more than 400,000 volumes each, and Liverpool and Leeds more than 300,000 volumes each. All these libraries were able to offer not only a full range of central reference, lending, and reading room services, but also a well articulated system of suburban branches, including, where appropriate,

89. THE BROWN LIBRARY AND MUSEUM, LIVERPOOL This handsome classical building, the gift of a wealthy Liverpool-Irish merchant, Sir William Brown, was opened in 1860. Additional buildings were added later. The terrace in front of the building has now alas been removed. *Radio Times Hulton Picture Library*

special provision for children. Manchester alone had twenty-three
branch libraries, eight branch reading rooms, and a number of delivery
stations.

Except at Manchester, accommodation for the central libraries was
on a generous scale. Liverpool had long been housed in a splendid
range of neo-classical buildings which included also the museum and
art gallery. Birmingham, after the tragic loss of its first central
library, and almost its entire reference collection, in a fire in 1879, had
promptly erected a new and larger building which was regarded
in its day as the finest of its kind in the United Kingdom. Leeds, from
1884, was handsomely accommodated in the new civic buildings.
Glasgow, though a comparative newcomer, had at its disposal both the
old and the new Mitchell Library buildings – the latter, opened in
1911, housing the reference library, while the former provided for the
central lending library.

Only Manchester was unlucky in this respect. Its first building,
the old Owenite Hall of Science, had to be evacuated in 1877 when
the weight of the growing library proved more than it could bear, and
the old Town Hall, to which the library was transferred, was de-
molished to make way for new development in 1912. At the outbreak
of the First World War, therefore, Manchester's central reference
library was housed in a group of wooden huts, in which it was destined
to remain for twenty-two years.

All these libraries now held impressive reference collections. Even
Leeds, which in the earlier years had dissipated much of its resources
on the multiplication of branch libraries in schools, could now offer a
reference library of nearly 100,000 volumes; and Glasgow and
Birmingham had more than twice that number. These great libraries
included many special collections on a variety of subjects. Always
there was a collection of material relating to local history and topography, and other special collections included the Burns Collection
at Glasgow, the Shakespeare Library at Birmingham, the Henry
Watson Music Library at Manchester, and the Hornby Art Library
at Liverpool.

In addition to these five libraries, there were about a dozen others
which by 1914 had accumulated total bookstocks in excess of 100,000
volumes, and may thus fairly be described as large libraries. Not all

91. TWO MAJOR
LIBRARIES
Above The Guildhall
Library, established
in 1828 as a repository
for material relating to
the City of London.
The building here
shown, completed in
1873 to the design of
Sir Horace Jones, was
used as a public re-
ference library until
1974. It was not at first
rate-aided, being
maintained until 1921
from the City's Privy
Purse. *Guildhall Lib-
rary*
Below The Mitchell
Library, Glasgow,
opened in 1911 and
still, with a substan-
tial recent extension,
the city's main refer-
ence library. *Glasgow
City Libraries*

of them, unfortunately, were in a position to render a first-class service: Sheffield, for example, was still hampered by a parsimonious civic administration; Edinburgh, in spite of its fine Carnegie building, was still labouring under the restriction of the penny rate; and the metropolitan boroughs of Westminster and Wandsworth were still struggling with the problems of divided administration resulting from the London Government Act of 1899 (the Act which created the metropolitan boroughs). One could, however, point to several other libraries in this group – Bolton, Bradford, Bristol, Cardiff, Dundee, Newcastle upon Tyne, Nottingham – which, often in spite of serious problems of finance and accommodation, were doing excellent work and contributing in a variety of ways to the development of the library service.

As these examples illustrate, as time went on and library stocks gradually increased there was a general tendency to build up special collections and develop a variety of specialised services. Even quite small libraries often sought to collect material of local interest, and the collections relating to local history and topography in some of the

92. TWO SMALLER LIBRARIES
Left The Gilstrap Library at Newark, presented in 1883 by Sir William Gilstrap, a local manufacturer and landowner: a contemporary sketch from Greenwood's *Public Libraries*, 1891.

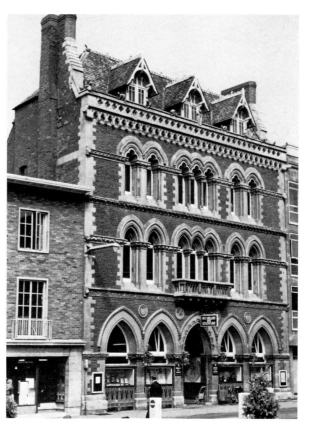

Right The library, art gallery and museum at Hereford, presented by Sir James Rankin in 1874: a pleasing example of Victorian Gothic by a local architect, Frederick Kempson. The building is still in use today. *Edith Kelly*

larger libraries were very impressive. The Norwich and Norfolk Collection at Norwich, for example, included manuscripts, books, pamphlets, newspapers and periodicals, theatre programmes, press cuttings, maps, engravings, lantern slides, photographs – everything that could serve to illustrate the life of the region, past and present. Other notable collections were held by Gloucester on Gloucestershire, by Plymouth on Devon and Cornwall, by Bradford on Bradford and Yorkshire. Special collections relating to local industries were also quite common, and in some libraries there were valuable collections, acquired often by gift or bequest, which had no special local relevance. Newcastle upon Tyne, for example, had a collection of Indian and Oriental works, Cheltenham a collection on fishes, while Swansea's special collections included not only, as might be expected, theology and Welsh history, but also the fine arts and modern European literature.

The most widely developed specialised service was that for children. Birmingham had from its beginnings in 1861 a juvenile section in every lending library, but at this time most libraries refused to admit readers under fourteen. It was only in the 'eighties, and largely as a result of Nottingham's example, that provision for children began to be extensively made. Samuel Morley, the Nottingham millionaire hosiery manufacturer and philanthropist, who afterwards gave his name to Morley College, took the initiative in the matter. Observing, as did so many of his reforming contemporaries, that 'everywhere in our large towns the working classes are deluged and poisoned with cheap, noxious fiction of the most objectionable kind', he concluded that the best antidote was the supply of wholesome literature to the young, and gave £500 to the public library for this purpose. The result was the Library for Boys and Girls, opened in 1882 in a building adjoining the central library, and with nearly 3000 books available for loan to children from seven to fourteen years of age. The librarian, J. Potter Briscoe, devoted a great deal of thought to this library and to what it should contain: the formula he arrived at was 50 per cent stories, 10 per cent magazines and annuals, and the rest mainly history, biography, travels, and popular science, with a little poetry and fine arts. In an address to the Library Association he stressed also the importance of having a librarian in charge who was sympathetic to children and accustomed to managing them.

Nottingham's example encouraged other libraries to experiment in this field. The idea of a separate children's branch did not often find favour, but it came to be widely accepted that children should be admitted to library membership and that special provision should be made for them. This was often done by allocating a special room for the purpose, or where this was not possible a special section of shelving.

93. THE NOTTINGHAM CHILDREN'S
LIBRARY, 1882
The building is now part of the Nottingham
University Extra-Mural Department. The
lady on the right was librarian-in-charge,
c. 1910. *Nottinghamshire County Library*

Occasionally – more as a social service than for library purposes – a
children's reading room was provided as well as a lending library.
Birmingham had a boys' reading room in the central library, and in
1902 the librarian, A. C. Shaw, related that on Sundays it would be
crowded to overflowing, with boys occupying every chair and
squatting in rows on the floor. He commented:

> It is not contended that they are doing much reading, as a rule
> probably they are not reading at all; they are of a class who are
> more interested in the illustrations than in the printed page, but
> even though this be the case the work that is being done is by
> no means to be despised.

As time went on, however, and the need to use the children's
library as an agency of social welfare diminished, the value of a
properly conducted reading room came to be more appreciated, and
a Library Association Conference in 1917 recommended that 'reading
rooms should be provided in all public libraries, where children
may read books in attractive surroundings, with the sympathetic and

tactful help of trained children's librarians'. Libraries also sought
to encourage the attendance of children, and to stimulate intelligent
reading, by lantern lectures, story half-hours, and organised visits by
school parties.

A number of authorities – Leeds and Norwich among them –
experimented during the late nineteenth century in the provision of
libraries in schools, but found the cost more than they could bear.
At Cardiff, however, where the librarian, J. B. Ballinger, made a
special feature of services for children, an arrangement operated from
1899 onwards under which the library organised a supply of books to

95. DELIVERY OF BOOKS TO A SCHOOL
AT BOOTLE
Each scholar was provided with a ticket,
and chose his own books from the printed
catalogue. The books were delivered
fortnightly in the 'neat covered hand-
cart' here shown, which bears the inscription: 'Bootle Education Committee.
Scholars' Book Delivery Dept. Central
Public Library.' The system was inaugurated in 1894, but this photograph
dates from the early years of the present
century. *Sefton Public Libraries*

every school, the teachers distributed them, and the School Board met the cost. This plan was imitated by a number of other librarians, notably by L. Stanley Jast at Croydon.

The extension of the public library service to hospital patients was to be a postwar development, but the provision of books for the blind began in the Liverpool lending libraries as early as 1857. Ten years

96. SCHOOL LIBRARY AT CARDIFF
Undated, but probably early twentieth century. *South Glamorgan Libraries*

CARDIFF EDUCATION COMMITTEE SCHOOL LIBRARY

earlier Dr William Moon of Brighton (himself blind) had formed a society to arrange the printing and distribution of the Bible and other works in the special type which he had invented. This was an embossed lettering, based on simplified forms of the conventional alphabet. The Moon system was for a time extensively used, and Liverpool and the handful of other public libraries which provided for the blind in the 'fifties and 'sixties held small stocks of books in Moon type. Later in the century, however, the British and Foreign Blind Association, after a careful study, gave its official backing to the now familiar Braille system, which had been invented by a Frenchman, Louis Braille, in 1834, and was based on embossed dots. This made it necessary for public libraries also to supply books in Braille, and the Manchester library at one stage employed several blind copyists in the making of Braille texts.

The difficulty about this kind of provision was that because of the high cost of production, and the large amount of shelf space required, only the largest public libraries could afford to carry a sufficiently large and varied stock to meet the needs of its blind readers. Eventually, therefore, it was found most economical to centralise provision through the National Library for the Blind, which was a voluntary body founded in 1882. From 1918 it had a Northern Branch in Manchester, which took over the stock formerly held by the Manchester public library. By arrangement with the Post Office, it was able to offer a post free service either direct to the individual reader or to a local blind institution. With generous help from the Carnegie Trust, the services of the National Library developed rapidly between the wars, and by 1925 it had a collection of over 100,000 volumes at its disposal. Two years later the Kenyon Committee's *Report on Public Libraries in England and Wales*, noting that 41 public libraries still had special collections for the blind, recommended that for the future 'any new scheme would probably best take the form of a subscription to the National Library'.

The lending of music scores was another special service in which Liverpool led the way, in 1859. Other libraries were quick to follow suit, for music was an important part of Victorian life. Choral and orchestral societies of all kinds flourished, and music-making was also popular in the home. By the end of the century many libraries, large and small, had music available for reference or for loan. Both sheet music and bound scores were in constant demand. By far the best collection of the time, and now one of the best in the world, was the Henry Watson Music Library at Manchester. When it was deposited at the public library by the donor (a local organist and composer) in 1900, it already numbered 16,700 volumes, and by the time of his death in 1911 it had increased to over 30,000.

Among the most obviously useful of the special services now provided by public libraries are those directed to the needs of local industry and commerce. Prior to the First World War these services were still little more than embryonic. In pursuance of the general policy of collecting material of local interest, many libraries had indeed accumulated considerable numbers of books relating to local industry and commerce, but these were not yet separately organised or purposefully directed to meet current needs. The first separately organised commercial libraries came during the war – at Glasgow in 1916, at Liverpool in 1917, at Bradford in 1918 – but the main development of such libraries, and of separately organised technical libraries, came only after the war.

97. LEADERS IN THE STRUGGLE OVER OPEN ACCESS
Left Alfred Cotgreave, Librarian of West Ham 1891–1905, and previously of Wednesbury and Wandsworth, an ardent advocate of the indicator system. *Newham Public Libraries*
Right James Duff Brown, who pioneered the open access system at Clerkenwell, where he was Librarian 1888–1905. From 1905 till his death in 1914 he was Librarian of Islington. His *Manual of Library Economy* (1903) was for a generation the standard guide to library management. *Islington Public Libraries*

Open Access

The most dramatic change in the public library service during these years was the introduction of open access for users of lending libraries. Hitherto, as we have seen, it had been a fundamental principle that readers must on no account be allowed access to the shelves. Cambridge and a few other libraries had indeed found it convenient to allow access to a limited number of reference works, such as directories, dictionaries, and encyclopedias, but everything else had to be hunted up in a catalogue and asked for over the counter. Now at last the barriers began to be swept away, and for the first time readers were allowed to select their books direct from the shelves.

The pioneer of this new system was James Duff Brown, librarian at this time of Clerkenwell, where the first experiment in open access was launched in May, 1893. A measure of control was still maintained, since the reader had to pass through a controlled wicket-gate on entry and again on leaving. This 'safeguarded open access' still operates in many libraries today, but the majority have now abandoned the wicket-gates and allow unimpeded entry and exit to all.

Even safeguarded open access, however, had its critics, the most vociferous being Alfred Cotgreave, who as the inventor of the Cotgreave indicator could fairly be regarded as having a vested interest in the maintenance of the existing system. Other librarians, however, were genuinely alarmed about the possibility of thefts, damage to books, and disorder among the readers. Feelings ran very high, and Berwick Sayers, afterwards chief librarian of Croydon, recalled that 'the municipal library profession went into two armed camps, and friendship and good feeling were frequently destroyed by it'.

Gradually, however, the new system spread, and experience showed that most of the fears expressed by librarians were groundless: the public were more honest, more orderly, and more intelligent than had been supposed. By 1910 about 70 libraries had adopted full or partial open access, and the major obstacle in the way of a more extensive use of the new system lay in the difficulties of conversion.

In the older libraries, and especially in the larger libraries, these difficulties were very great. When the public was excluded the books could be stored in lofty bookstacks, reaching up to the ceiling if necessary, and packed closely together, and they could be shelved simply in numerical order within a few broad categories such as History, Philosophy, Literature, Science. Once the public was admitted, however, it became necessary, first, to reduce the height of the bookstacks so as to bring all the shelves within the reader's reach; second, to provide adequate circulation space between the stacks;

98. THE TRUTH ABOUT
OPEN ACCESS
Above Frontispiece to an
anonymous pamphlet of
1895, *The Truth about
giving Readers Free Access
to the Books in a Public
Lending Library.*
Below The Chorlton-
cum-Hardy Branch,
Manchester, opened
1914, showing 'safe-
guarded open access'.
Entry to the lending
library at the rear is
through a turnstile beside
the issue desk. A similar
turnstile on the other side
controls exit. *Manchester
City Libraries*

and third, to reclassify the books, and re-label the shelving, in such a way that the reader could find for himself the books that he needed. All these changes involved not only time and money, but also a great deal more space. It is not surprising to find, therefore, that even in progressive libraries conversion often had to await the opportunity provided by new building or large-scale reorganisation.

Reclassification was a major headache for big libraries. Brown, at Clerkenwell, began by introducing sub-divisions into the main existing classes, for example under Natural and Mathematical Sciences he had sub-divisions for Botany, Chemistry, Geology, Zoology, Astronomy, Mathematics, and so on. Later he produced, on this basis, a new and more detailed system of classification, which in its fully developed form was known as Brown's Subject Classification. This system, because it was relatively easy to adopt, became for a time quite popular, especially with the smaller libraries, many of which continued to use it until after the Second World War. Eventually, however, the classification that carried the day, and is now almost universal in the public libraries of this country, was the Dewey Decimal System, devised by the American Melvil Dewey in the 1870s and based on ten main subject classes, each represented by a three-figure number:

000	General Works	500	Natural Science
100	Philosophy	600	Useful Arts
200	Theology	700	Fine Arts
300	Sociology	800	Literature
400	Philology	900	History

Each of these classes had nine divisions numbered 1–9, and each division had nine sub-divisions also numbered 1–9. Should a further breakdown be needed, additional sub-sections could be created to whatever extent seemed desirable by additional figures following a decimal point, thus creating a hierarchy of subject divisions:

900 History
  940 European History
    942 History of Great Britain
      942·1 History of London
        942·19 History of Middlesex

The system was flexible, in that it could be adopted in whatever degree of detail was useful in a particular library; it was almost infinitely sub-divisible to accommodate new subjects; and with the addition on each volume of a few letters to indicate the author's name, it made it simple to arrange the books on the shelves in an orderly sequence which could be followed by any reader of average

Opposite
99. SOME EARLY LIBRARY BOOKPLATES
Early public library bookplates represent a fascinating and little explored field of study, well illustrated by these four contrasting examples, all from the turn of the century.

intelligence. With these virtues it is not surprising that by 1910 Dewey was already rivalling Brown in popularity. Now, after a hundred years, and in spite of weaknesses due to the passage of time, it is so firmly established as to be almost immovable.

Professional Training

All these developments made it increasingly necessary for library staff to have some kind of training. The earliest public librarians were essentially amateurs: some, but by no means all, had had some previous experience of librarianship, in mechanics' institutes or subscription libraries, but none had any training. The best of them, however, did very well, growing with the job, and in the larger libraries training up a body of assistants from whom in due course came the librarians of the future. From 1877 the Library Association, founded 'to unite all persons engaged in or interested in library work', provided the opportunity for public librarians to meet each other, and to meet their colleagues from non-rate-aided institutions such as the British Museum and the university libraries, to compare experience and consider common problems. Even though the public library element in the Association was at first very weak, this was a hopeful sign.

Gradually the nature of a librarian's duties, and the qualifications required of librarians at different levels, became better defined. In 1880 the Library Association started its first professional journal, and two years later it launched its first scheme for professional certificate examinations. The response at this stage was not good: lack of time, lack of money, and lack of teaching were all serious obstacles in the way of the young library assistant in search of qualifications. Classes, summer schools, and correspondence courses began to be provided in the 'nineties, and J. Macfarlane's *Library Administration*, published in 1898, was the first of what was to be a long series of textbooks for the guidance of students. The best known of them was to come five years later. This was James Duff Brown's *Manual of Library Economy*, which was to be for more than half a century the *vade mecum* of the aspiring librarian. Its publication in 1903 was a landmark in the development of library training, and in the very next year the Library Association launched a much more sophisticated scheme of certification, involving examinations in six subjects –

literary history; bibliography; classification; cataloguing; library history and organisation; and library administration.

In 1909 the Library Association was able to take the important step of establishing an official register of librarians, in which the main professional grades were fellowship (FLA) and membership (MLA). Librarianship was at last on its way to becoming a profession, and the effect was dramatically seen in a number of libraries when for the first time a qualified librarian was appointed.

This happened at Winchester following the appointment of A. C. Piper in 1914. Although this was the first public library to be opened under the 1850 Act, it was still at this time very backward, with an annual expenditure of £40 on books and binding and £55 on periodicals. Within seven years Piper reorganised the entire library, extending the building, reclassifying and recataloguing the stock, and making the books available for the first time on open access.

A similar story unfolded at Norwich, another very early library, which first advertised for a qualified librarian in 1911. It is significant that there were 110 applicants, out of whom the committee selected G. A. Stephen, Chief Assistant Librarian at St Pancras. The library was one which had made good progress in the nineteenth century, but since 1901 two incompetent librarians in succession had created an appalling condition of neglect and stagnation. Stephen reported that both building and books were dirty, and did not seem to have been cleaned for years – the fiction stock, indeed, was so filthy as to be a menace to health. In the reference library only the local collection was of value, the remaining stock being 'quite inadequate to meet the requirements of students and businessmen'. There was no staff room, no office, no files of correspondence. In the library's own bindery two repairers were engaged 'on patching dirty books that were beyond repair and in botching other books in a way that would lead to their rapid destruction'.

With the backing of the committee Stephen at once took in hand the immense task of reorganisation. The building was cleaned and re-decorated, and regulations drawn up for its use. The bookstock was thoroughly weeded and replenished, reclassified and recatalogued, the new catalogue being published in sections in a periodical *Readers' Guide*. A special catalogue was published for the local collection, which was enriched by the inauguration of a press-cutting service and a photographic survey of Norwich and Norfolk. For the first time a library service was organised for children. The staff were given notice to undertake training and examinations – in fact most of them resigned. All this was accomplished within a few years. By 1920 Norwich was already one of the foremost libraries in the country, and in that year reorganisation was completed by making the lending library available to readers on open access.

Changes such as these clearly foreshadowed the new and improved library service that was to come.

100. NINETEENTH-CENTURY READER'S TOKEN
Bradford was a pioneer in methods of recording loans. The 'pocket' system still used in many lending libraries, in which a card is transferred from a pocket in the book to a pocket in the reader's ticket, was invented there in 1873. Readers in the reference library were issued with a numbered metal token (here illustrated), so that they did not have to write out their names and addresses every time they needed a book. *Bradford Public Libraries*

Further Reading

Most of the works on general library development cited at the close of the previous chapter are also relevant here, but for much interesting detail it is necessary to turn to other sources. The Parliamentary Returns of Public Libraries, published in the Parliamentary Papers at intervals between 1853 and 1912, should not be neglected: the earliest returns (1853, 1856, 1857, 1870, 1876, and 1877) include a great deal of useful information and comment. Much may also be learnt from J. D. Brown's *Manual of Library Economy* (1903, 2nd edn. 1907), which is concerned with all aspects of library management. On the open access controversy see W. A. Munford, *James Duff Brown, 1862–1914: Portrait of a Library Pioneer* (Library Association 1968).

For details of individual libraries it is necessary to browse in reports of Library Association conferences (published in various forms since 1879); in library periodicals, especially the *Library World* (from 1898–99) and the official *Library Association Record* (from 1899); and in local library histories. These last are numerous but mostly in ephemeral pamphlet form. The most substantial, all published by the libraries concerned, are: Butler Wood, *A Brief Survey of the Bradford Libraries, 1874–1922* (1922); T. W. Hand, *A Brief Account of the Public Libraries of the City of Leeds, 1870–1920* (1920); Peter Cowell, *Liverpool Public Libraries: a History of Fifty Years* (1903); W. R. Credland, *The Free Library Movement in Manchester* (1895); G. A. Stephen, *Three Centuries of a City Library* [Norwich] (1917); Philip Hepworth and Mary Alexander, *City of Norwich Libraries: History and Treasures* (1957, reprinted with other material in *City of Norwich Libraries*, 1965); and *The City Libraries of Sheffield, 1856–1956* (1956). Among recent pamphlet histories those dealing with Birmingham (1962), Cambridge (by W. A. Munford, 1955), Glasgow (1955, 2nd edn. 1966), Newcastle upon Tyne (1950), and Oxford (1954) are of particular interest.

Towards a National Service   4

The End of the Penny Rate

By 1914 it can fairly be said that Great Britain had the beginnings of a national library service. It was, however, patchy in its distribution and uneven in its quality – in some places very good, in some very poor, in some non-existent. And although many libraries kept before themselves the ideal of serving the whole community, the service was still in practice directed mainly towards the needs of the urban working class. If the service was to become truly national and comprehensive a number of changes were necessary:

> 1 Public libraries must be given adequate resources. This meant, in the first instance, the abolition of the 1d rate limitation, but ultimately it called for the creation of larger and more efficient library authorities.
> 2 The service must be extended to rural as well as urban areas.
> 3 The concept of libraries for the working classes must give way to the concept of libraries for all.
> 4 Adequate arrangements must be made for an interlending service, so that each public library could call on the services of all.
> 5 A link must be forged between the local public libraries and libraries of national standing such as the British Museum and the National Library of Scotland.
> 6 All libraries must be under the direction of competently trained staff.

A great step towards the achievement of the first two objectives came with the Public Libraries Act of 1919. This was in large measure a consequence of the First World War. During the war prices more than doubled, and this brought library finance, already strained, to crisis point. The government was at first unsympathetic, and evidently regarded public libraries as expendable. An official circular of 1915 recommended local authorities to examine library expenditure carefully 'with a view to possible economies', and many authorities were only too happy to comply: after all, working people had more important things to do during a war than reading. Quite often library buildings were commandeered for war purposes. The City of Westminster, at the end of the war, had only one of its four buildings still operating, and even that was working with reduced hours.

By 1919, therefore, the position of the libraries was desperate. From all over the country urgent representations were made to the Board of Education. Because of the penny rate limitation, it was stated, libraries were 'wholly unable to pay any war bonuses to their staff', and many were 'actually unable to buy any new books'. E. A. Savage, librarian at Coventry during the greater part of the war, summed up the state of affairs in his usual vivid way:

> From 1914 Government raked up all our money to wage war, prices rose steeply, our income was slashed. By the time the relief Act was passed in 1919 all town libraries had dirty leavings of bookstocks in their lending rooms. Stores were choked with books to bind or replace. Buildings were in shabby disrepair, some hardly weather-tight. Librarians, never without gold coins in their pockets in 1914, were near the bread-and-soup line.

At the same time, as we shall describe later, pressure was building up for legislation to permit county authorities to operate public library services. Eventually in November, 1919, a government bill was introduced covering both these points, i.e. the removal of the rate limitation and the extension of library powers to the counties. It was passed before the end of the year, though not without opposition. Sir Frederick Banbury, spiritual successor to that Colonel Sibthorp who had fought against the 1850 Act, declared his belief that public libraries were 'places, where, if the weather is cold, people go in and sit down and get warm, while other people go in to read novels'. Such libraries, he believed, had done more harm than good, 'because the books read, as far as my information goes, are chiefly sensational novels, which do no good to anybody'.

This Act applied only to England and Wales. In Scotland the counties had already secured permission to provide a library service

Opposite:
101. BRADFORD CENTRAL LIBRARY, 1922. I
These and the two succeeding photographs may be regarded as fairly typical of a medium-sized urban library in the early 'twenties. On the whole the facilities available were not very different from those available before the war.
Above The Lending Library, not enclosed by indicators but still without open access.
Below The Newspaper Room.

under a clause in the Education (Scotland) Act of 1918, but the non-county authorities continued to be restricted to the penny rate until 1920, when the Public Libraries (Scotland) Act raised the limit to 3d.

In spite of the new legislation, improvement came only very slowly. The tradition of penury in the library service was deeply ingrained. Even in 1924, when the overall price index stood at 139 compared with 85 before the war (it had been up to 251 in 1920), nearly 70 per cent of library authorities in England and Wales were levying a rate of 2d or less, and 35 per cent were still levying less than 1d. The situation was not helped by the economic collapse of 1922, and the consequent drastic cuts in public expenditure. It was not until about 1926 that the outlook began to be a little brighter.

Two major reports surveyed the position as it was in the early 'twenties. The Mitchell Report, on *The Public Library System of Great Britain and Ireland, 1921–23*, was prepared for the Carnegie Trust by its Secretary, Lieut-Col J. M. Mitchell, and published in 1924. The Kenyon Report, on *Public Libraries in England and Wales*, was prepared for the Board of Education by a Departmental Committee under the chairmanship of Sir Frederic Kenyon, Director and Principal Librarian of the British Museum. It was published in 1927, but the statistics on which its conclusions were based related mainly to 1923–24. Apart from the introduction of the county library service, neither report was able to record any dramatic improvement over the position revealed in the Adams Report of 1915.

Few new urban authorities were created at this time. The only notable exceptions were in London, where the last three metropolitan boroughs – Paddington, Bethnal Green, and St Marylebone – commenced service in 1920, 1922, and 1923 respectively. Paddington, however, adopted only to avoid a takeover by the London County Council, and provided no more than a minimum service until 1930. Building, too, was at a low ebb, and the Carnegie Trust, though continuing to honour old promises, announced in 1922 that it was not prepared to consider new applications for grants towards building costs. A few new branch library buildings were erected here and there, but hardly any new central libraries.

The shortage of books continued, too, and in the smaller libraries the ill-paid and often ill-qualified staff spent much of their time patching and pasting to make the books last a little longer. Some still ran subscription libraries to augment their scanty stock. The Kenyon Report recommended that trained librarians should be on a salary

Opposite :
102. BRADFORD CENTRAL LIBRARY, 1922. II
Above The Magazine Room, with Reference Library beyond.
Below Study carrels in the Reference Library – an unusual feature.

scale comparable with that paid to trained teachers, but it had to admit that many existing librarians were quite unfitted for their posts, and it cited one authority which employed at £2 a week an official who acted as 'Cleaner, Caretaker, Stoker, Borough Librarian and Secretary to the Committee'.

There were, however, some gains to be recorded. Libraries continued to grow, albeit slowly; branch organisation continued to develop; and many of the larger town libraries, following the lead given by Glasgow during the war, began to provide special commercial and technical libraries to meet the needs of the business and industrial classes. Open access also made steady headway: it was now standard practice in all new buildings, but older buildings often required extensive reconstruction – at Birmingham in 1923 the central lending library, with 40,000 volumes shelved on wall presses 26 feet high, had to be closed for five months to make conversion possible. In most cases the introduction of open access was accompanied by reclassification and recataloguing on the Dewey Decimal system, the old printed catalogues being discarded in favour of the now familiar card or sheaf catalogue, which was very much easier to keep up to date.

Special provision for children was now becoming normal, and at Manchester from 1919 onwards the young people's reading rooms created by L. Stanley Jast set a new standard for this work. The schoolroom atmosphere characteristic of earlier children's reading rooms was deliberately eschewed: instead there were small tables,

103. CARD CATALOGUE AT THURROCK
The card catalogue, introduced into this country from the United States in the late nineteenth century, became increasingly popular with the advent of open access, and is still a firm favourite in most libraries. The photograph shows the catalogue for the Adult Lending Library at Thurrock's new Central Library, opened in 1972. *Essex County Library*

104. OXFORD JUNIOR LENDING LIBRARY, 1921
The Oxford Central Library, occupying at this time cramped accommodation in the Town Hall, could find room for a children's library only in the basement, where it remained until 1927. *Oxfordshire County Libraries*

105. THE NEW STYLE CHILDREN'S READING ROOM
The Grangetown Branch at Cardiff. *South Glamorgan Libraries*

separate chairs, and books in gaily coloured jackets in low bookcases, with flowers, pictures, lectures, talks and story reading to add to the attractions. In the building of new branch libraries it now became common for the lending library to be made the central feature, with an adult reading room on one side balanced by a juvenile library on the other side.

On the professional side a hopeful sign was the establishment in 1919, with assistance from the Carnegie Trust, of the School of Librarianship at University College, London, which for the first time offered a full-time training course. Graduates could take the Diploma in Librarianship in one year, non-graduates in two, and there were also facilities for part-time study. As at Norwich a decade earlier, the importance of professional skills was again exemplified in the reforms carried out by R. J. Gordon and J. P. Lamb, successive librarians at Sheffield in the 'twenties. Once again, by energetic and informed management, a notoriously backward and inefficient library was cleaned up, restocked, recatalogued, reorganised, and converted into a thoroughly modern and forward looking service with, needless to say, all the advantages of open access.

The Beginnings of the County Service

One of the most important recommendations made to the Carnegie Trust in the Adams Report of 1915 was that experiments should be undertaken in the provision of books to rural areas. Under existing legislation, as has already been mentioned, the counties had no powers to act as library authorities, and although rural villages could and not infrequently did assume library powers they lacked the resources to provide an adequate service. For the most part, therefore, the rural areas, when they had any library service at all, had to depend upon privately supported schemes.

Village reading rooms, supported from the funds of the well to do, were not uncommon, for example in the Midland counties; and there were various schemes for the periodical exchange of bookboxes on the plan first used by Samuel Brown at Haddington earlier in the century. Yorkshire had its Village Library, operating on this plan, under the auspices of the Yorkshire Union of Mechanics' Institutes; Suffolk had its Village Clubs Association, Dorset its Schools and Villages Book-lending Association, Hereford its circulating libraries, the Isle of Wight its Seely Library. This last was founded in 1904 by Sir Charles Seely, who gave £5000, more than 10,000 books, and an endowment of £100 per annum, to establish in Newport a lending library and reading room open to all inhabitants of the island. He also arranged for small collections to circulate among the villages.

He placed the scheme under the management of the County Education Authority, and it eventually became the starting point for the county library.

Rural libraries in many parts of the country also drew on the help of a body known as the Central Circulating Library, which had its headquarters in Liverpool. This was a voluntary organisation, originally intended to serve local needs. For a subscription of a guinea a year it supplied thirty books, changed three times a year.

In Scotland, at the beginning of the present century, James Coats of Paisley, a member of the well known thread manufacturing family, distributed small libraries – usually 300 or 400 books in a lock-up bookcase – to hundreds of rural parishes in Scotland, especially in the Highlands and Islands, but since no provision was made either for exchange or for renewal these quickly lost their usefulness.

As soon as the Adams Report became available the Carnegie Trustees set to work to implement its recommendation concerning rural libraries. They began by providing funds, wherever appropriate, to reinforce existing schemes. For the North of Scotland they actually provided additional books to strengthen the Coats libraries, sending from their headquarters at Dunfermline boxes of about 75 books,

106. JAMES COATS OF PAISLEY Founder of the Coats Libraries. In addition to providing libraries for Scottish villages, Coats sent books every New Year's Day to every lighthouse in Scotland, together with two pipes and 2 lbs of tobacco. *Renfrew District Library*

exchangeable every six months, to more than a hundred centres in Orkney, Shetland, and Lewis. For the inhabitants of the Hebrides, only cheap editions were provided, since books read in the peat smoke atmosphere of the ill-ventilated 'black houses' soon had to be destroyed.

The next stage, which began in 1916, involved new schemes devised within the framework of existing legislation. One relied upon a grouping of rural library authorities round an urban authority which would act as a centre for the distribution of books. Worksop in Nottinghamshire was the first such centre, and similar arrangements were later developed based on Montrose, Perth, and Grantham. Another and more successful plan, known as the Staffordshire scheme and later adopted in a number of English and Welsh counties, relied on persuading the County Education Committees to use their powers in relation to elementary schools to provide bookboxes for all schools in rural areas, 'principally for the children in attendance at the schools, and also for other inhabitants in the villages'. This second plan could not be operated in Scotland, but the green light for county provision there was given by the Scottish Education Act of 1918, which empowered county education authorities

> as an ancillary means of promoting education, to make such provision of books by purchase or otherwise as they may think desirable, and to make the same available not only to children and young persons attending schools and continuation classes in the county, but also to the adult population resident therein.

The corresponding English Education Act made no similar provision, but in the agitation leading to the 1919 Public Libraries Act the Carnegie Trust pressed very strongly, not only for the removal of the rate limitation, but also for the extension of library powers to county authorities, and this proposal was, in fact, accepted. The Act provided that a county council might adopt the Public Libraries Acts for such part of the county as it thought fit, excluding only county boroughs and districts in which a public library service had already been inaugurated. It also provided that library matters should be controlled, not, as in the urban areas, by a separate library committee, but by the education committee or a sub-committee of the education committee. This structural difference was to have a significant effect on the development of the county library, which was from the first seen quite specifically as a part of the educational service.

The acceptance of the proposal for a county library service probably owed much to the general concern, at this time, over the condition of the countryside. For a long time British agriculture had been in decline − a decline only temporarily halted by the war-time expansion of demand. Low wages, geographical situation, poor housing, and poor social and educational facilities, all contributed to make the countryside a depressed area, and to encourage a drift of population to the towns. The county libraries were one element in a general movement for rural rehabilitation in which the Women's Institutes (initiated in Wales in 1915), the Village Clubs Association, the Rural Community Councils, the Rural Industries Bureau, the Village Drama Society and other organisations all played their part. All these bodies had come into existence by 1921. Later came the Rural Music Schools (1929) and the first of the Cambridge village colleges (1930). By this time, however, the motor-car, the motor-bus, and the radio had done much to break down the old isolation, and bring the villages more into touch with urban amenities.

In order to ensure, as far as possible, that the county authorities took advantage of the new legislation, the Carnegie Trust offered grants in aid of the capital cost of books and equipment (not buildings, since special buildings were deemed unnecessary). Modest as these grants were, they served their purpose, and by the end of 1927 most counties had at least commenced a library service. The only exceptions were, in England, Westmorland (which had an arrangement with Kendal), Holland in Lincolnshire, Rutlandshire, and the Scilly Isles; in Wales Carmarthenshire; and in Scotland Argyllshire. Only Rutlandshire, the Scilly Isles, and Argyllshire were still without a service on the eve of the Second World War.

Unfortunately the Carnegie Trustees, in their anxiety to see county libraries started, had set their sights very low. They envisaged little more than a service of bookboxes to country villages, and encouraged authorities to think in terms of a rate of $\frac{1}{10}$d or less. The service provided was, in consequence, even more rudimentary than that provided seventy years earlier by the first municipal libraries: usually a box of 50–100 books for each village, deposited in the local school and with the schoolteacher acting as voluntary librarian. The books were commonly exchanged three times a year. After a few years some counties tried to break with the school tradition by establishing centres in village halls, women's institutes, and the like, but for a long time centres in schools predominated.

Any old building, for example a disused barn or army hut, would serve as headquarters accommodation, provided only it had an office for the librarian and shelving for the few thousand books not actually in circulation. If the librarian had a clerk to help him in the task of making up and sending out the bookboxes he could count himself fortunate. Distribution was at first normally by rail or carrier's van − in Orkney and Shetland often by boat − but some authorities soon

107. EARLY LIBRARY VANS

Above Kent County Library van, 1926–27. The first motorised travelling library was brought into use by the Perthshire County Library in 1920. In England Kent was the pioneer. Both used vans of the type shown here, which served as shop windows from which those who were in charge of village centres could select their own stock. Access was from the outside only, as in the horse-drawn vehicle used by Warrington Mechanics' Institute and illustrated on p. 69. Lindsey County Library, in 1925, first introduced an interior access van, which gave protection from the weather.

Below Middlesex County Library van, 1928. This type of van – basically a delivery van, with racks to carry trays of books – was also widely used. *Harrow Libraries* began to hire motor transport, or even acquire their own library vans. When this happened, however, the librarian often had to drive the van himself. In Lindsey, where a chauffeur was engaged, the van was equipped with a folding table and a portable typewriter so that the librarian might improve the shining hour by dealing with his correspondence *en route*.

The main demand among readers, inevitably, was for fiction, and a typical bookbox would contain half adult fiction, one-quarter juvenile fiction and the rest non-fiction. There were never enough books, and in 1925 the West Riding County Library reported that it was not uncommon for a borrower, finding the shelves completely empty, to have to wait for another reader to turn up with a book.

On the other hand the new county libraries, just because they were under the auspices of the education authorities, made special efforts to cater for educational demands. Some inherited teachers' libraries, previously kept at the Education Office, and the tendency was for these to be broadened out into students' libraries open to all serious readers. This service was separate from that at the village centres, the books being kept at headquarters and made available either to personal borrowers or by post. A beginning was also made in providing school libraries, and special pains were taken to provide books for adult classes, plays for literary and dramatic societies, and music for musical societies. In this attention to educational needs the county libraries were almost from the beginning in advance of all but the best of the non-county libraries.

As time went on the county libraries began to grapple with the problem of the urban areas within their boundaries, which had initially been excluded from consideration. They included small market towns and industrial and mining communities, together with suburban areas which had grown up outside the boundaries of the larger towns. These were areas which had not themselves adopted the Libraries Acts, but it was impossible to provide for them on the village bookbox system. What was needed was a branch system of the kind developed by the urban libraries, and in many areas this was achieved by a differential rating system, the local authority concerned agreeing to pay an extra rate, over and above the normal library rate, in return for the provision of some kind of branch service, for example a reading room and lending library. Under the Scottish local government system differential rating was not possible, but some counties none the less found ways and means of establishing branch libraries in urban areas. Midlothian opened its first urban branch at Musselburgh in 1925. In England the first purpose-built county branch was opened at Ashford in Kent in 1927.

Progress and Difficulties

By 1926 the worst of the postwar depression was over, and the public libraries began to look towards a more hopeful future. Many of the non-county libraries, shaking themselves free at last from the tradition of the penny rate, embarked upon ambitious schemes of modernisation, involving for example the introduction of open access, the overhaul and reclassification of stock, the replacement or improvement of buildings, increased branch provision, and better service for children. A sign of the times in 1927 was the adoption of the Libraries Acts at Hastings – the last county borough to adopt. The county libraries, steadily moving towards a wider concept of service, signalised their emergence as an important factor in the cultural life of the community by the adoption in 1928 of a special county library sign, a red torch on a cream background, which was installed at the cost of the Carnegie Trust outside some 15,000 library centres.

These bright hopes were roughly dashed by the great world depression which began in 1929 and was at its worst during the years 1931–33. Libraries were forced to suspend their plans for expansion and in many cases to cut back their services, and urban reading rooms filled up once more, as in so many depressions in the past, with sad rows of unemployed. In some places the practice of blacking out the betting news had to be reintroduced.

During these grim years the Carnegie United Kingdom Trust gave modest but invaluable assistance. Though the trustees had now terminated their building grants, they made available between 1926 and 1936 grants totalling £138,600 to improve bookstocks in

108. THE COUNTY LIBRARY SIGN
This sign, designed by fifteen-year old Philip Colman of the Bradford College of Arts and Crafts, was long a familiar feature of village life.

some of the smaller non-county libraries – always, of course, on condition that steps were taken to improve the efficiency of the service. They also continued to make grants to the county libraries, particularly to encourage their efforts to make provision for urban areas. Another factor that helped to temper the severe financial climate was an agreement reached in 1929 under which booksellers agreed to supply books to public libraries at a discount, subject only to a minimum annual expenditure. For libraries spending £500 a year or more (from 1932 £100 a year or more) the rate of discount was 10 per cent.

At length the clouds rolled away, and by the mid-thirties the libraries were beginning to enjoy what Savage afterwards looked back on as a 'little summer of prosperity before 1939' – a prosperity which took tangible form in an increase of 45 per cent in local government expenditure on libraries and museums between 1933 and 1939. The opening of handsome new central libraries in Manchester, Sheffield and Birkenhead, all in the year 1934, marked the opening of a new period of building and reconstruction. The new library in Manchester, with its great circular reading room, was particularly welcome after more than twenty years spent in wooden huts.

109. HENDON CENTRAL LIBRARY, 1929
Designed by T. Millwood Wilson, and completed just before the onset of the great depression, this pleasant building in the Georgian style was one of the few library buildings erected during the 1920s.

110. MANCHESTER
CENTRAL LIBRARY,
1934
This classical building
by E. Vincent Harris
was the major library
building of the inter-
war years. The ex-
terior is shown above,
the Great Hall below.
The bookstacks, artifi-
cially lighted, were in
the centre of the
building, below the
Great Hall, so that the
various library rooms
round the circumfer-
ence of the building
had the advantage of
natural lighting. The
departments sur-
rounding the Great
Hall are shown on the
plan opposite: others
included the Music
Library, the Foreign
Library, the Central
Lending Library, and
a basement Lecture
Hall which after the
Second World War
was developed into
a Library Theatre.
*Manchester City
Libraries*

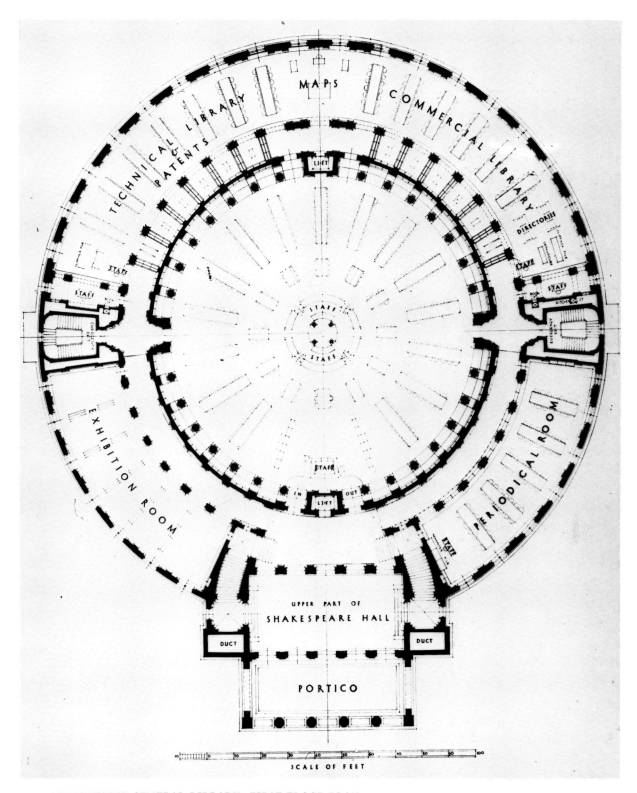

III. MANCHESTER CENTRAL LIBRARY: FIRST FLOOR PLAN
The Great Hall, pictured opposite, is in the centre of this floor, lighted from above.
Manchester City Libraries

112. THE PICTON LIBRARY, LIVERPOOL, 1936 The resemblance between this splendid room, erected in 1879 and the Great Hall at Manchester is obvious. Probably both rooms owe something to the great circular Reading Room at the British Museum (see p.179). The Picton Library was designed as a students' reading room, and was named in honour of Sir James Picton, Chairman of the Liverpool Library Committee. *British Library*

The larger county library systems were now advancing apace. By 1938–39 Lancashire and the West Riding held bookstocks of more than 400,000 volumes each, and in Lancashire issues had topped the four million mark. Other large county systems were Kent, Durham, Surrey and Middlesex, and in Scotland, Lanarkshire and Ayrshire. Good headway was made with the development of branch service in the urban areas, and the clumsy differential rating system began to give way to uniform rating, which made possible more effective overall planning. The Carnegie Trust, in spite of the fact that it was now running down its assistance to libraries, made a special grant of £25,000 to help with provision for new housing estates.

Housing developments, combined with improved transport facilities, were also a matter of concern to many urban libraries. What was happening, as one speaker pointed out at a library conference in 1935, was 'a disintegration of the old grim compactness of works, streets, shops and houses'. Large numbers of people, no longer compelled to live in the shadow of their workplaces, moved out to new homes in the suburbs, often to new houses built amid the green fields. The old inner city branches became redundant,

The Middlesex County Branch at Ruislip, opened in 1937 in the reconstructed fifteenth-century barn of the old manor farm.

and it was not always easy to find the money to build new ones further out – the Carnegie grants were made only to the county authorities.

An innovation which was to prove of benefit to both urban and rural libraries was the mobile library. This was in effect a small branch library on wheels, with interior shelving from which the readers could choose their own books, and a small issue desk. It carried about 1000–1200 books. This type of library was first introduced in Manchester in 1931 to cope with the problem of the new housing estates on the fringes of the city. Other urban authorities copied the idea, and in the counties mobile libraries came into use extensively both as substitutes for the old static village centres and to provide a direct service to isolated hamlets and homesteads.

In general the picture of library development on the eve of the Second World War was very uneven. The best authorities were now giving a wide-ranging and efficient service, but there were still too

114. EARLY MOBILE
LIBRARY
One of Manchester's
first mobile libraries,
converted from a
single-decker bus.

many small and inefficient authorities. Many of the smallest, it is true, had now been absorbed by the counties, or in some cases by neighbouring towns. In Scotland parish libraries had been compulsorily absorbed into the county structure under the Local Government (Scotland) Act of 1929. There still remained, however, a total of more than six hundred library authorities in Great Britain, and the service given by many of these was very poor indeed, either through sheer inefficiency or because they were too small to be viable.

The weaknesses of the situation show up very clearly in a survey conducted for the Library Association in 1936–37. The Association's observers noted many large libraries (Birmingham and Cardiff were notable examples) struggling to give a twentieth-century service in all too solid nineteenth-century buildings; and many small libraries which, although they might have buildings, had little else. In the West Riding of Yorkshire 10 out of 45 non-county libraries were serving populations of less than 10,000: only two of these had trained librarians, and most were giving little more than newsroom service. In the Cheshire–Shropshire–North Wales area 50 out of 56 libraries visited fell into the category of small libraries, in which those in charge were usually caretakers. Of the smaller libraries of South-West Scotland–North-West England (from Glasgow to Barrow in Furness) the observer wrote severely:

There was a dreary sameness about all the buildings. A stuffy staleness and an odious smell of disinfectant pervaded nearly all of them . . . Dark olive green shelving was in use in the majority of libraries . . . The book stocks throughout the area were in a woeful condition – dirty, out of date, laden with germs, dog-eared, and without any attraction whatsoever . . . Generally the 'reference library' consisted of a bookcase containing an old edition of an encyclopaedia and a few old tattered copies of dictionaries.

Some of the county libraries also came under criticism. In Scotland some were too small to provide an independent service, and three had part-time librarians. In South Wales and South-West England it was reported that:

One county library is housed in the disused cells of a prison; one in old army huts; one in a temporary wooden structure; four in houses, or parts of houses, converted to library use; three only in suitable premises; and of these three, two have outgrown their present accommodation . . . In three cases the staff at headquarters consisted of the librarian and his assistant.

We may digress here for a moment to refer to the miners' institute libraries which were such a distinctive feature of the South Wales scene, and were the subject of brief but critical comment in the report. The miners' institute movement dated in the main from the 1890s, when the 'Free Education Act' of 1891 made it possible for miners to

115. FOUNDING FATHERS The foundation committee of the Tredegar Workmen's Institute, 1890. *South Wales Miners' Library*

116. TREDEGAR
MINERS' LIBRARY,
1962
Note the bust of
Aneurin Bevan in the
foreground. By this
time interest in public
libraries of this type
was declining, and
within two years the
Tredegar library was
dispersed. Most of
the 23,000 books have
been lost. *Western
Mail and Echo*

116. TREDEGAR
MINERS' LIBRARY,
1962
Note the bust of
Aneurin Bevan in the
foreground. By this
time interest in public
libraries of this type
was declining, and
within two years the
Tredegar library was
dispersed. Most of
the 23,000 books have
been lost. *Western
Mail and Echo*

divert to the building and maintenance of such institutes the weekly
pence which they had formerly contributed to provide elementary
education for their children. By 1914 nearly every large mining
community had its institute, with the library and reading room as a
central feature. From 1920 onwards the Miners' Welfare Commission
provided funds for the building of welfare halls, also with libraries,
in the smaller centres.

These libraries, ranging normally up to about 15,000 volumes,
were comparable to those of the nineteenth-century mechanics'
institutes. Tredegar in Monmouthshire, which has been described as
'the classic institute in the inter-war period', grew to over 20,000
volumes, for a community of 10,000 people. Its library committee,
we are told, whose chairman in the early 1920s was Aneurin Bevan,
'spent £300 per annum on books, of which £60 was set aside exclusively for the philosophy section'. This institute had been founded
in 1890 by workmen of the Tredegar Iron and Coal Company, who
contributed ½d a week each from their wages; shop assistants were
allowed to join at 6½d a quarter, and tradespeople at 1s 6d per quarter.

The achievement of the miners' institute libraries has been rightly
praised, but by the 1930s they were standing in the way of the development of a more efficient public service. County libraries were able to
salve their consciences by providing a few hundred volumes from

117. READING ROOM AT
THE OAKDALE INSTITUTE,
MONMOUTHSHIRE
South Wales Miners' Library

118. SELECTING A
BOOK IN A MINERS'
LIBRARY
An unidentified
photograph from the
mid 'thirties. *South
Wales Miners'
Library*

time to time to supplement institute supplies; and in some of the larger communities the establishment of an independent library service was delayed. Rhondda did not commence library service till 1939, Mountain Ash not till 1964.

From South Wales to London seems a far cry, but the London libraries, too, came under criticism in the Library Association report, attention being drawn particularly to the weakness of the reference service and the lack of technical and commercial libraries.

A remark which Edward Sydney, Librarian of Leyton, made in relation to the West Riding libraries sums up the position for the whole country:

> The advance guards are well out in front, the main body is in touch yet a little slow, but there are far too many stragglers in the rear slowing down the pace of the whole column.

Libraries for All

It is not possible to pinpoint the precise time at which the concept of libraries for the working classes gave way to the concept of libraries for all. The change took place at different times in different authorities, and indeed, within different sectors of the same authority. Generally speaking, the better and more comprehensive the service, the sooner the transition came. It was the major reference collections in the big city libraries which first broke the working-class barrier: even in the nineteenth century, as we have seen, these libraries were attracting readers from many different social groups. Lending libraries, and branch libraries concentrating mainly on lending and reading room provision, were much more proletarian, and in general the small town library was more working-class than the large town library. The reading room was lowest of all in social estimation, and was often avoided even by people who used other sections of the same library.

None the less the Kenyon Report of 1927 marks an important stage in the transition. Here for the first time, in an official government document, the doctrine of libraries for the working classes is abandoned in favour of a wider concept of usefulness. A few passages from the Report are worth quoting:

> Even now we should not venture to say that the possibilities of the public library are always adequately recognised. It is not long since the reproach that public libraries existed mainly for the supply of indifferent fiction for the poorer classes had too much truth in it to be easily repelled. But with the coming of the second generation brought up under the system of universal education the conception of the use of books has widened. Commerce and industry have learnt, more slowly in this country than in America, but still have learnt, that study and research are essential, not merely for progress but for survival in the struggle for existence. The war of 1914–18 brought home this necessity with irresistible force, and few would now deny that if a crowded industrial population, such as that of Great Britain, is to continue to hold its own, it can [do so] only by the utilisation of its best brains and by the application of all the resources of knowledge and intellectual culture.

> The public library should be the centre of the intellectual life of the area which it serves. That intellectual life covers all stages, from the incipient curiosity of those whose intelligence is only beginning to awaken to the advanced research of the highly-trained specialist. The library has to serve not only the earnest seekers after knowledge, but also those who are merely gratifying an elementary curiosity, and those who are seeking relaxation and recreation . . .

> The principle underlying the library service is that it exists for the training of the good citizen. It must aim at providing all that printed literature can provide to develop his intellectual, moral, and spiritual capabilities . . .

The librarian aims, therefore, at supplying recreational literature of as good quality as his public can digest; at placing at their disposal the information necessary for the ordinary duties of a citizen; and at supplying all their needs for intellectual culture and for the knowledge that they require in their several professions and occupations . . .

Several objectives for library work are mixed up here – education, recreation, information for industry and commerce, support for the researcher, training for citizenship – but none of these objectives is associated in any way with social class. The idea of the library as the intellectual centre of its area probably derived from a remark by W. C. Berwick Sayers, librarian of Croydon, in his third edition of Brown's *Manual of Library Economy* (1920): 'The object is to make the library the intellectual centre of the town.'

There is, however, one other passage in the Kenyon Report which shows that the old idea of providing for the lower orders was still not quite dead. In dealing with the choice of fiction, the Report recommends libraries not to be in too much of a hurry to buy new books:

> A few months' delay will weed out a very large proportion of them and will allow the influence of careless or interested criticism to evaporate. The needs of those who require the newest books while they are new are sufficiently catered for by the subscription libraries.

It has to be recognised that the commercial subscription libraries, especially the giants of the trade, such as Mudie's, W. H. Smith's, Boot's, and the Times Book Club, did much to preserve class distinction in library use. Those who could afford it naturally preferred to get their fiction, and the lighter kinds of non-fiction, clean and fresh, and it was only as conditions in the public libraries improved, and financial pressures on the middle classes increased, that the distinction was gradually broken down. The depression of 1931–33 had some effect, and the oldest of the great circulating libraries, Mudie's, founded in 1842, disappeared in 1937.

In this same year the concept of libraries for all was clearly and unequivocally stated by Lionel McColvin of Hampstead, one of the great librarians of his generation. In a little volume on *Libraries and the Public* he declared:

> . . . The public library should serve all who can use it, and it should be all-embracing and free from partisanship or bias of any kind.
>
>   . . . Those who suggest that the public library is, or is not, for

119. LIONEL MCCOLVIN
Librarian first of Ipswich, then of Hampstead, and finally, from 1938 to 1961, of the City of Westminster, Lionel McColvin was one of the outstanding librarians of his generation. He was for seventeen years Honorary Secretary of the Library Association, and his one-man 'McColvin Report', published in 1942, had a profound effect upon future library development. *Westminster City Libraries*

any particular class, deny [this principle]; those who fail to cater, as well as they may, for the research worker or the semi-illiterate in the slums, for the student or the businessman, the parson or the poet, do not live up to it.

There are many reasons why we should insist that the public library is for all. All support it, through the rates; the services it renders may be of use to any or all and there is no good reason why they should not be given where they can be valuable; what is good for one man, one class, one age, one type of vocation, can, with necessary modifications, be good for another; the things in which we deal – facts and ideas – are of significance to all . . .

A number of factors contributed to this gradual change of attitude. One was the improvement in library buildings, as the old fashioned Victorian buildings, with their dark colours and solid mahogany furniture, began to give way to more modern buildings. Lighter colours for paintwork, new flooring materials such as rubber and linoleum, larger windows, improved lighting, and the occasional use of plants, flowers, and pictures, all helped to create a brighter and more welcoming atmosphere. Open access was, of course, now the rule in all new or reconstructed buildings, and many libraries found it possible to dispense with the barriers which had once been looked on as an essential safeguard. Book displays, or displays of book jackets, became a common factor.

The additional space needed for open access and book displays was found by reducing the amount of space allocated to reading rooms and newsrooms, which because of the general improvement in working-class housing were less necessary than they had once been. Often, in old libraries, the reading room and the lending library were interchanged. Because of the emancipation of women, separate ladies' reading rooms also ceased to be regarded as essential, and when reconstruction took place such rooms were often converted into children's libraries. In county library branches, of course, reading room accommodation was exceptional, and separate accommodation for ladies was unknown.

Another factor making for change was the steady increase in the range and variety of library services, for readers of all ages. Provision for children, now almost universal, was in many libraries a particularly attractive feature, supported by story hours, play-readings, discussion groups, lantern lectures, even in some places films. County libraries followed suit, and in their new branches began to provide a children's room or at least a children's corner. Close relations were established with schools, especially elementary schools. Classes of children visited the library for lessons, and both urban and county libraries frequently assumed responsibility for providing libraries in schools: among urban libraries Cardiff, Edinburgh and Hull were particularly active in this field.

Just before the war a few libraries were making special provision for adolescent readers between fourteen and seventeen. This kind of service, pioneered at Walthamstow in the 'twenties, was a gallant attempt to check the loss of readers in the years immediately after leaving school (the minimum school-leaving age at this time was fourteen). Unfortunately the practice never became widely established.

Local history and other local studies continued to receive a great deal of attention, and much was done, especially in the larger town libraries, to improve service to the industrial and commercial community. Liverpool, for example, had a commercial library in the main business quarter, some distance from the central library. It provided books, directories, reports, periodicals, maps, and other useful material, and maintained special indexes of articles in commercial periodicals. Sheffield had from the opening of its new library in 1934 a Commercial Library and also a Library of Science and Technology, and through the initiative of its librarian, J. P. Lamb, was linked with the University library and a variety of specialist

Written in Friars' Carse Hermitage —

Thou whom chance may hither lead,
Be thou clad in russet weed,
Be thou deckt in silken stole,
Grave these counsels on thy soul. —

Life is but a day at most
Sprung from night, in darkness lost,
Day, how rapid in its flight,
Day, how few must see the night!
Hope not sunshine every hour,
Fear not clouds will always lour. —

As Youth and Love, with sprightly dance,
Beneath thy morning-star advance,
Pleasure with her siren air
May delude the thoughtless Pair:
Let Prudence bless Enjoyment's cup,
Then raptured sip & sip it up.

As thy Day grows warm & high,
Life's meridian flaming nigh,
Dost thou spurn the humble vale?
Life's proud summits would'st thou scale?
Check thy climbing step elate,
Evils lurk in felon wait:
Dangers, eagle-pinioned, bold
Soar around each cliffy hold,
While cheerful peace with linnet song
Chants the lowly dells among. —

As thy shades of evening close,
Beckoning thee to long repose;

120. LOCAL HISTORY IN THE PUBLIC LIBRARY
From the very beginning public libraries have interested themselves in the historical, literary and artistic associations of their areas, and many have now accumulated rich collections of printed, manuscript, and pictorial material. These two examples are from Glasgow:
Left Autograph poem by Robert Burns, 'Written in Friars' Carse Hermitage', from the James Cowie Collection.
Right Castle Street and the Cathedral Tower in the 17th century: one of the pictures from the Glasgow Room. *Glasgow City Libraries*

libraries belonging to industrial firms and research organisations. Such specialist libraries, each dealing in detail with some fairly restricted branch of knowledge, were now becoming numerous, and since 1924 had their own organisation, known as ASLIB (Association of Special Libraries and Information Bureaux). Local cooperative organisations such as that established at Sheffield (still flourishing today under the title SINTO – Sheffield Interchange Organisation) were therefore specially valuable, and were to become numerous after the war.

It was at this time, too, that public libraries began to develop 'out-

121. THE BEGINNINGS OF SERVICE TO INDUSTRY AND COMMERCE
Above A businessman takes his problem to the Information Desk at the Cardiff City Library, *c.* 1920. *South Glamorgan Libraries*
Below The Commercial Library at Bradford, 1922. Opened in 1918, this was one of the first libraries of its kind in the country. *Bradford Libraries*

reach' services to readers in hospitals and prisons. Hospital libraries originated in the provision made by the Red Cross and Order of St John for sick and wounded soldiers during the First World War, and it was not until 1930 that the Library Association began to concern itself with this work. In the following year a special committee of the Association recommended that a library service should be established in hospitals throughout the country, and that this service should be a responsibility of public library authorities. Not all libraries, however, had the resources needed to take the initiative in this matter, and not all hospitals were ready to welcome such an initiative. Progress was therefore at first rather patchy, and where service was provided it was by a mixture, in varying proportions, of public and voluntary effort. In few cases was the service under full professional direction.

It was not until 1936 that the Library Association began to concern itself with the prison library service. At its suggestion, the Prison Commissioners agreed to the appointment of a panel of librarians to advise on suitable books for the libraries which were customarily provided for the use of prisoners; and by 1939 a few public libraries had established direct contact with their local prisons and were beginning to give some kind of assistance.

An increase in library extension activities might also have helped

122. THE LEYTONSTONE BRANCH LIBRARY
This Branch, opened in 1934, was the centre for Edward Sydney's many and varied extension activities. It is noteworthy not only because of the wide range of accommodation provided but also as a very early example of a library built over shops – an economical way of achieving a central position. *Waltham Forest Libraries*

123. SOME OF LEYTONSTONE'S
EXTENSION ACTIVITIES
(*See also below, p. 237*)
Above A gramophone record
recital, conducted by a member
of the library staff. *Central Office
of Information*
Below Play by the library's
Junior Group, in rehearsal.
Central Office of Information

to widen the range of library use, but few authorities, at this period, had either the will or the resources for any large expansion on this side of their work. The now traditional types of extension work continued – lectures, exhibitions, story hours for children, encouragement to local cultural societies, loan of books to adult classes. Many librarians also showed themselves eager to cooperate, from the late 'twenties onwards, in the formation of 'wireless listening groups', meeting on library premises to hear and discuss BBC radio talks, though in the end this movement had to be written off as a failure. On the whole, however, librarians were less than enthusiastic about the Kenyon Report's vision of the public library as the intellectual centre of the community.

One of the few who did accept this ideal wholeheartedly was Edward Sydney, librarian of Leyton. His branch at Leystonstone, opened in 1934, included not only the usual library rooms but also a lecture room and two classrooms, and the equipment available included showcases and exhibition screens, blackboard, piano, lantern, epidiascope, film unit, radio and gramophone. The library served as a meeting place for local authority classes and more than a score of cultural and educational societies, and the library's own activities included a music club, lectures, discussion groups, plays and play-readings, and art exhibitions. Translating the Kenyon ideal into practical terms, Sydney urged, in an article published in the *Year Book of Education* for 1938, that the public library should be 'the headquarters of all local cultural activities', and should be equipped for the purpose.

The Beginnings of Inter-Library Cooperation

For the development of a truly national library service, adequate arrangements for inter-library lending were essential. Links had to be forged not only between the local public libraries, supported by the rates, but between these and the national libraries which were maintained by the central government.

The oldest and greatest of these was the British Museum Library, founded in 1753, and designed 'for the use of learned and studious men'. It embraced many famous collections of books and manuscripts, including the Royal Library, presented by George II in 1757, and a second royal collection, the King's Library, presented by George IV in 1828. It also had the great privilege, which it shared with the Bodleian Library at Oxford, the University Library at Cambridge, the Advocates' Library in Edinburgh, and Trinity College Library, Dublin, of receiving free of charge one copy of every book published in the United Kingdom. The law of copyright deposit, which still

124. MONTAGU HOUSE, GREAT RUSSELL STREET,
ORIGINAL HOME OF THE BRITISH MUSEUM
From a drawing by T. H. Shepherd. *British Museum*

125. THE BRITISH
MUSEUM READING
ROOM OF 1838
From a drawing by
T. H. Shepherd.
British Museum

126. SIR ANTHONY
PANIZZI
Chief Librarian of
the British Museum,
1856–66. From the
portrait by
S. Gambardella.
British Museum

applies today, went back to 1662, and at one time as many as eleven libraries were included in the list, but in 1836 the number was reduced to the five just named.

By the twentieth century the main problem of the British Museum Library was to accommodate its vast holdings. The most famous of its librarians, Sir Anthony Panizzi, who held office from 1856 to 1866, had built the great circular reading room in the vacant central quadrangle of the Museum building, with shelving round about it for a million volumes. Within thirty years, however, the new accommodation was already under pressure, and various later additions, including a newspaper repository at Hendon, gave only temporary relief. In the inter-war years, with each year's new accessions requiring about a mile of shelving, the Library was engaged in a constant struggle to cope with the ever-increasing flood of material.

Cataloguing, too, was a serious problem. Panizzi had initiated an alphabetical author catalogue on manuscript slips which were pasted into folio volumes and could be rearranged when necessary. When this grew to more than 2000 volumes, and threatened to take over the entire reading room, it was replaced by a printed catalogue, which was published in 1905 and covered accessions to 1900. A new catalogue,

127. THE BRITISH MUSEUM
READING ROOM OF 1857
Above The great circular reading
room, conceived by Panizzi and
opened during his term as librarian,
is still the main reading room of the
British Library (now known as the
British Library Reference Division). The picture gives an artist's
impression about the year 1902.
Liverpool University
Below A surviving sector of the old
'Iron Library', surrounding the
reading room and constructed at
the same time, photographed in
1928. *British Library*

begun in 1931, made slow progress: by the end of 1939 it had reached its twenty-ninth volume and still had not got beyond the letter B.

The National Library of Wales, a product of Welsh national pride and zeal for learning, received its charter in 1907, and opened in temporary premises in Aberystwyth two years later, with John Ballinger, formerly librarian of Cardiff, as its first librarian. It moved to its permanent home, splendidly situated on a hillside overlooking the town of Aberystwyth, in 1916, though the building was not completed until after the Second World War. The special mission of the Library was to collect material of Welsh interest, and thanks in part to generous donations it had by 1926 already acquired practically every important printed work in Welsh since 1546, besides rich manuscript collections. Under the Copyright Act of 1911 it became, with certain limitations, a copyright deposit library.

The National Library of Scotland had been founded by the Faculty of Advocates in Edinburgh in 1680. Its scope was always wider than the law, and it soon became a centre for material relating to Scottish history and literature, freely accessible for reference to all scholars. It became a copyright library in 1709, and this privilege eventually created a situation in which the Faculty could no longer face the cost of maintaining such a large public collection. In 1926, when the library was transferred to the nation, it comprised about 750,000 books and pamphlets, as well as important manuscript material. A new building was badly needed, and was actually begun in 1938, but the outbreak of war soon brought operations to a halt.

Other important national collections included the Victoria and Albert Museum Library, a specialist library of the literature of art which had its beginnings in connection with the Government School of Design in 1837; the Science Museum Library, particularly strong in scientific periodicals, which traced its origin back to the needs of the Geological Survey in 1843; and the Patent Office Library, opened to the public in 1855, which contained not only English and foreign patent material but a wide range of scientific and technical literature.

It was, however, a much more modest library which became the starting-point for what was eventually to become an all-embracing scheme of national library cooperation. The story goes back to 1903, when Albert Mansbridge, a London cooperative worker and University Extension student, founded the Workers' Educational Association, which at once embarked on the provision of classes for adult workers. From 1908 the Association collaborated closely with the universities in the promotion of part-time 'tutorial classes', which extended over three winter sessions and required a high level of commitment by the student. It was to meet the needs of these classes that

129. THE NATIONAL LIBRARY OF WALES, ABERYSTWYTH, 1937 Originally designed by S. K. Greenslade, this impressive building was brought to completion in a modified form, by Charles Holden. The similarity in outward design to the National Library of Scotland (pictured below, p. 209) which was begun in 1937, is very noticeable. *National Library of Wales*

the WEA, in collaboration with Toynbee Hall, London, established in 1912 a small Central Library for Tutorial Classes.

The Carnegie Trust, recognising the wider possibilities of this library, provided funds in 1916 for its transformation into an independent organisation known as the Central Library for Students. Five years later the Trust established a Scottish Central Library for Students in Dunfermline. By 1927, when the Kenyon Report was published, both libraries were giving a useful service as libraries of last resort for requests from other libraries. The Central Library for Students, at this time, had a stock of 37,000 volumes at its Bloomsbury headquarters, and was in addition able to draw on the stocks of forty 'outlier libraries', including many specialist collections. It was making 50,000 issues a year, of which 20,000 were going to county libraries, 15,000 to non-county libraries, 2000 to other libraries, 11,000 to adult classes, and 2000 direct to individual borrowers. The Scottish Central Library for Students, as might be expected, was operating on a smaller scale.

The Kenyon Report, which it will be remembered was restricted in its remit to England and Wales, saw the Central Library for Students as the keystone in a national cooperative structure. At the base of this structure would be the local public libraries, grouped together in a system of voluntary cooperation round regional centres. These, it was thought, would normally be the great urban libraries, the county libraries at this time being too weak to discharge such a responsibility. Demands which could not be met at regional level would be passed to a reconstructed Central Library for Students, which would have access, it was hoped, not only to the resources of other regions, but also to those of university and other specialist libraries. The new Central Library, it was suggested, should be a special department of the British Museum, supported by a substantial government grant. The Museum should also be asked to establish a Central Cataloguing Agency, to supply catalogue cards for new publications to libraries throughout the country, and thus eliminate much unnecessary duplication of work in individual libraries.

Though the Museum declined to accept these new responsibilities, steps were eventually taken to carry out the Kenyon Report's major proposals. In 1931 the Central Library for Students was reconstructed as the National Central Library, with a small annual grant from the government to enable it to act as a central bureau of library information. In 1933 it moved to more commodious premises in Malet Place, provided by the Carnegie Trust. It continued to supply books to adult classes, and to a very small extent to isolated individual students, but its main task now was to act as a clearing house for library interlending and as a source of supplementary supply. In this task it was

This adapted build-
ing in Malet Place,
with the Library
Association conven-
iently next door,
served the National
Central Library for
thirty-two years, in
spite of considerable
damage during the
war. In 1965 the
building was taken
over by University
College, and the
Library was trans-
ferred to new premises
near by.

soon able to draw on the support not only of its outlier libraries but
also of a network of eight regional library bureaux established between
1931 and 1937.

These bureaux, which absorbed a number of earlier and more
local cooperative schemes, brought together in each region public
libraries, university libraries, and many special libraries. They acted
as local agencies for interlending, passing to the National Central
Library only requests which could not be met from within the region.
The running costs were met by the member libraries, but the Carnegie
Trust subscribed more than £260,000 towards the preparation of
'union catalogues' to facilitate the location of books.

The eight regions were: Northern, North-Western, Yorkshire,
Wales, West Midlands, East Midlands, South-Western, South-

Eastern. The Northern Bureau was located at the Newcastle upon Tyne Literary and Philosophical Society, the South-Eastern Bureau at the National Central Library, the Welsh Bureau at the National Library of Wales, the others in major public libraries. The Scottish Central Library for Students carried out similar functions for Scotland till a bureau was eventually established there in 1945. London was outside the regional system, but had a union catalogue of the Guildhall and metropolitan borough libraries, and a system of interlending covering most of these libraries.

Thus during these inter-war years a number of important steps had been taken towards the development of a national library service. Except in the Scottish burghs (where a 3d rate persisted) rate limitation had everywhere been abolished; rural as well as urban areas were now covered; the concept of libraries for all was steadily taking hold; and the framework had been created for a national cooperative interlending system.

131. REGIONAL
LIBRARY BUREAU
AREAS, 1936

REGIONAL LIBRARY SYSTEMS OF ENGLAND & WALES.

Further Reading

Most of the general works cited in connection with previous chapters are still relevant for the inter-war years. For this period we also have available a number of important official reports. J. M. Mitchell, *The Public Library Systems of Great Britain and Ireland, 1921–1923* (Carnegie U.K. Trust, Dunfermline 1924) was a sequel to the Adams Report of 1915. The *Report on Public Libraries in England and Wales* (Cmd. 2868, 1927) prepared by the Public Libraries Committee of the Board of Education, and better known as the Kenyon Report, is the first full-scale Government assessment of the library service; and L. R. McColvin (ed.), *A Survey of Libraries: Reports on a Survey made by the Library Association during 1936–37* (Library Association 1938), provides a detailed and often brutally frank commentary.

The great new feature of this period is the advent of the county library service, which may be studied in K. A. Stockham (ed.), *British County Libraries, 1919–1967* (Deutsch 1969), and also in a contemporary work, E. J. Carnell, *County Libraries: Retrospect and Forecast* (Grafton 1938). The county libraries were a special concern of the Carnegie U.K. Trust, whose *Annual Reports*, beginning with that for 1913–14 (Dunfermline 1915), provide detailed information concerning their origin and development. Much of value may also be gleaned from the published proceedings of the periodical County Library Conferences which were sponsored by the Trust from 1920 onwards; and for those interested in statistics there are numerous reports published first by the Trust and later (from 1929) by the Library Association. For the non-county libraries the only comparable publication was *Statistics of Urban Public Libraries in Great Britain and Northern Ireland (1935)* (Library Association 1936).

For the development of library organisation and techniques successive editions of J. D. Brown's *Manual of Library Economy* (3rd edn. Grafton 1920, 4th edn. 1931, 5th edn. 1937, all edited by W. C. B. Sayers) are still the main guide. For this period they may be supplemented by B. M. Headicar, *A Manual of Library Organisation* (Allen and Unwin and Library Association, 1935, 2nd edn. 1941); J. M. Mitchell (ed.), *Small Municipal Libraries: a Manual of Modern Methods* (Library Association 1931, 2nd edn. 1934); and A. S. Cooke (ed.), *County Libraries Manual* (Library Association 1935). See also E. A. Savage, *A Librarian's Memories, Portraits and Reflections* (Grafton 1952); W. G. Fry and W. A. Munford, *Louis Stanley Jast: a Biographical Sketch* (Library Association 1966); and W. A. Munford, *James*

Duff Brown, 1862–1914: Portrait of a Library Pioneer (Library Association 1968).

Three items from the thirties reflect an increasing awareness of public relations in library work. They are: L. R. McColvin, *Libraries and the Public* (Allen and Unwin 1937); Eric Leyland, *The Wider Public Library* (Grafton 1938); and L. S. Jast, *The Library and the Community* (Nelson 1939).

The standard history of the British Museum Library is A. J. K. Esdaile, *The British Museum Library: a Short History and Survey* (Allen and Unwin 1946); but G. F. Barwick, *The Reading Room of the British Museum* (Benn 1929), makes more entertaining reading. See also Edward Miller, *Prince of Librarians: the Life and Times of Antonio Panizzi of the British Museum* (Deutsch 1967). The only other items of substance on the history of the national libraries are W. Llewellyn Davies, *The National Library of Wales: a Survey of its History, its Contents, and its Activities* (National Library of Wales, Aberystwyth 1937); and B. Houghton, *Out of the Dinosaurs: the Evolution of the National Lending Library for Science and Technology* (Bingley 1972).

Periodical literature becomes increasingly varied and important during these years. From 1928 a convenient guide is to be found in the annual volumes published by the Library Association under the title *The Year's Work in Librarianship*, Vol. I appearing in 1929.

The Second World War and After

5

Libraries under Fire

During the First World War public libraries had been looked upon by the government as fit subjects for economy. During the Second World War, a war which it was recognised from the first would involve civilians at home as well as troops on the fighting front, the Board of Education called upon all local authorities to maintain and if necessary extend the services offered by public libraries, which by affording recreation and instruction for vast numbers of readers, and by providing centres for the organisation of cultural activities, could materially assist the national war effort. Instead of being merely a period of retrenchment, therefore, these troubled years from 1939 to 1945 offered to the libraries new opportunities for service.

There were, of course, difficulties. Money was scarce; staff (both men and women) were called into the armed forces or some other form of wartime service; books became increasingly difficult to get; accommodation was sometimes commandeered for emergency purposes; senior staff were often involved in additional duties as air raid wardens, information officers, and the like; streets were blacked out and transport facilities reduced; and at some periods there was a considerable shift of population, especially children, from London, the ports and the big industrial centres into rural areas less vulnerable to enemy attack. About fifty central or branch libraries were actually destroyed, or very badly damaged, by direct enemy action, amongst them the central libraries at Coventry, Exeter and Plymouth, and the central lending library at Liverpool. The National Central Library and the British Museum Library also suffered serious damage, as did the Hendon Newspaper Repository. In all some 750,000 books perished.

It was amid such difficulties that the public libraries set to work to meet the many challenging demands that now faced them. To deal

Opposite :
132. WARTIME DESTRUCTION I
Above Part of the old 'Iron Library' which surrounded the British Museum Reading Room: 200,000 volumes were destroyed. *British Library.*
Below The British Museum Newspaper Library at Hendon: 30,000 volumes of newspapers were destroyed. *British Library*

with what was described as an unprecedebted demand from civilian readers they adjusted their opening hours and where necessary created temporary branch libraries and other service points. They shuttled books backward and forward between town and country to meet the needs of evacuees, and eased their regulations regarding the inter-availability of library tickets. They made special arrangements for the loan of books to H.M. Forces and assisted in the building up of unit libraries, which as time went on became increasingly important in connection with Forces educational schemes. They monitored a National Book Recovery Campaign which produced not only millions of books for H.M. Forces but also about 650,000 books and a large number of periodicals which were eventually used, after the war, for replacement of stocks in war damaged libraries at home and abroad. They supplied books to Air Raid Wardens' posts, First Aid posts, Auxiliary Fire Service stations, and other civil defence centres; during the heavy air raids of 1940–41 they even provided small libraries, staffed by volunteers, for the thousands of people who crowded nightly into London's underground shelters. In collaboration with the war-time Ministry of Information, and the newly established Council for the Encouragement of Music and the Arts, they also organised lectures, displays, exhibitions, films, plays and concerts, on a scale never previously envisaged.

All these activities made the public more aware of the role that public libraries could play in community life, and helped to prepare the way for postwar developments. The form that these developments might take was explored by Lionel McColvin, City Librarian of Westminster, who in 1941 was commissioned by the Library Association to survey the present condition and future needs of the public library service. As Honorary Secretary of the Library Association McColvin was in an excellent position to undertake this task, and the report he presented, in the autumn of 1942, made a dramatic impact.

His analysis of the current position, though more thorough and incisive than the Library Association survey of 1936–7, pointed to many of the same weaknesses, and especially to the immense disparity between the best and the worst. He paid more attention, however, to professional matters, for example the confusion of classification and cataloguing systems, and the shortage of qualified staff. He was specially critical of the recently introduced regional library bureaux. The

133. WARTIME DAMAGE II
Above Burnt books like slices of charred toast on the shelves of the National Central Library. Most of the Library was destroyed in April, 1941. *British Library*
Below Damage at Bethnal Green Central Library, September, 1940. *British Library*

134. CARRYING ON
Above Lending library at Bethnal Green tube station air raid shelter, where in 1941–42 a library of 4000 books was serving a nightly clientèle of 6000 people. *British Library*
Below The wartime Travelling Library lent to St Pancras for the duration of the war by Hastings Public Library. *Fox Photos*

interlending system, he pointed out, was slow, cumbersome and expensive: it would be cheaper to buy books, wherever possible, than to provide them through the bureaux, and for out of print books a single national centre would be the most efficient agency.

The most revolutionary section of the report was that which set out McColvin's proposals for the future. The simplest way to secure a more efficient library service, he argued, was to create larger library units, and he actually produced a map showing the existing 604 library authorities of the United Kingdom reduced to 93. The City of London and the 28 metropolitan boroughs made up 9 units, the rest of England 69, Wales 5, Scotland 9, Northern Ireland 1. Ignoring the distinctions between town and country, he tried wherever possible to ensure that each unit should embrace 'a normal natural congregation of people', but since he regarded a population of about 300,000 as the minimum for an efficient service, his map showed one authority covering the northern half of Scotland, and another covering three-quarters of Wales.

These new library authorities, McColvin suggested, should be under the direction of a central government department – perhaps the Board of Education or a Ministry of Fine Arts. They would be subject to government inspection but would also be eligible, like other sectors of local government, for government grant. Up to this time, it should be noted, government control over the public libraries had been minimal. The right to approve loans, exercised under the original 1850 Act by the Treasury, had now passed to the Board of Education, which also had a measure of control over the county libraries by virtue of the fact that they were subordinate to the county education committees. The Kenyon Committee had considered, but firmly rejected, proposals for government grant and control, arguing, perhaps rather disingenuously, that an atmosphere of freedom was an essential condition of healthy library progress. This argument McColvin ruthlessly brushed to one side.

On the basis of the new and larger library authorities, McColvin proposed to erect a new and more efficient structure of inter-library cooperation. The new authorities would be expected to acquire all general standard works, and each would be allocated a subject or subjects in which it would be expected to acquire not only standard works, but also more specialised and expensive material. Inter-library loans would thus be restricted to specialist works and out of print standard works. The regional library bureaux could be dispensed with, and the National Central Library, relieved of many of its responsibilities for inter-library lending, would be free to develop as a central agency for bibliography and cataloguing.

McColvin also made detailed recommendations regarding the

training and remuneration of staff. The Kenyon Report, fifteen years earlier, had pointed out that to create an effective career structure in librarianship it was necessary to provide for different grades of work and different levels of salary, and that in large libraries there were many duties of a routine kind which did not call for a professional training. In 1933 the Library Association had gone some way towards implementing this suggestion by abolishing its six professional certificates in favour of a graduated system involving Elementary, Intermediate and Final Examinations. McColvin's ideas were on similar lines, but in order to provide for the training of professional staff on the scale required by the new libraries he stipulated that five or six additional library schools should be established in the larger provincial centres.

Many librarians were deeply shocked by McColvin's proposals, and it was only with considerable misgivings that the Association agreed to publish the Report. Nevertheless when in 1943 the Association published its own *Proposals for the Post-War Reorganisation and Development of the Public Library Service* it accepted in principle all McColvin's major recommendations, even the proposal for larger library units. It was, however, anxious to avoid the creation of *ad hoc* library authorities, preferring to pin its hopes on a general reform of local government which would produce 'areas suitable not only for libraries but for education, public health and most, if not, indeed, all other local government purposes'. In this matter the Association showed good judgment, but more than thirty years were to pass before the dream became reality.

The Battle of the Boundaries

It was hardly to be expected that the smaller library authorities would accept without a struggle proposals under which, in the interests of efficient service, they would lose their independence and be merged in new and larger authorities. So long as the war lasted the struggle was muted, but at the first postwar conference in 1946 the Library Association's recommendation concerning library areas was voted down and had to be withdrawn.

The proposal that the whole of the North of Scotland should form a single library area aroused particularly fierce opposition, and in 1945 the Scottish Library Association (now in union with the main Association) decided to make its own assessment of the position. Not surprisingly C. S. Minto, Deputy Librarian of Edinburgh, who was commissioned to make a new survey of the ten northern counties, was more generous in his judgment than McColvin had been, but even he was compelled to recognise the weakness of the small burgh

libraries. His report, *Public Library Services in the North of Scotland,* published in 1948, recommended that these small independent libraries should be merged with their respective counties, and that some of the less populous counties should join forces with their neighbours, but by and large his proposals left the county structure intact. A policy statement by the Scottish Library Association, appended to the report, accepted that an adequate library service could not normally be organised by an authority with a population of less than 20,000. This was, it may be recalled, the figure which had been put forward by the Kenyon Committee, twenty years earlier, in respect of the libraries in England and Wales.

In the meantime the Secretary of State for Scotland had decided on an official inquiry. The resulting report, the McClelland Report on *Libraries, Museums and Art Galleries,* was published in 1951, and came to the conclusion that an efficient library service could not be provided for a population of less than 30,000. The simple solution recommended was that library powers should be exercised only by education authorities, i.e. by the counties and the four cities (Aberdeen, Dundee, Edinburgh and Glasgow). The burghs were at once up in arms, and in the event the recommendation was not implemented. The Public Libraries (Scotland) Act of 1955 removed the anomalous 3d rate limit on the burgh libraries, but otherwise did little to improve the efficiency of library service.

In the same year the Library Association again came forward with proposals for reform. This time they took rateable value as a guide, and suggested that the library powers of authorities with a rateable value of less than £300,000 should be surrendered to the counties, but again the smaller libraries voted the proposal down. There was indeed some voluntary surrender of powers to the counties and the larger urban libraries. About forty of the weakest library authorities, mostly in England and Wales, disappeared in this way during the late 'forties and 'fifties. This did something to improve the situation, but the basic problem remained.

In an endeavour to solve it, the government in 1957 appointed a special committee, under the chairmanship of Dr S. C. Roberts, Master of Pembroke College, Cambridge, 'to consider the structure of the public library service in England and Wales, and to advise what

136. READING ROOMS

Reading rooms of the old kind still survived in many smaller urban libraries, especially in the industrial areas, and were still popular with working-class readers. The upper picture is from a library in the West Riding, *c.*1948. *British Library*; the lower picture, which demonstrates that rest as well as recreation was still one of the purposes of a reading room, is from a library in the North-West, 1958. *Guardian*

changes, if any, should be made . . .' The Committee had no difficulty in agreeing that counties, county boroughs, metropolitan boroughs, and the City of London should continue to be library authorities, and that parishes should cease to be library authorities. In respect of authorities intermediate between these two groups, i.e. the non-county boroughs and urban districts, the Committee received, as might be expected, much conflicting advice, but eventually, following a line suggested by the Library Association, adopted a criterion which took into account not only population but also library expenditure. The Roberts Report, published in 1959, recommended that existing non-county borough and urban district library authorities should be allowed to continue subject to a minimum annual expenditure on books of £5000, or 2s per head of population, whichever was the greater. New authorities in this category, however, would be considered for recognition only if they had a population of at least 50,000.

The Report made a number of other recommendations, for example for the improvement of staffing and premises, for a statutory system of inter-library cooperation, and, most important of all, for government supervision of the library service. The government accepted most of the recommendations, but set up two working parties to explore in further detail (a) the basic requirements for an efficient library service, and (b) the machinery for inter-library cooperation.

The first of these working parties produced in 1962 a valuable report on *Standards of Public Library Service in England and Wales*, with detailed recommendations regarding staffing and premises, lending and reference services, children's services and general cultural activities. In place of the criteria of efficiency proposed by the Roberts Committee, related to annual expenditure on books, it suggested criteria related to the number of books purchased. An efficient library, it suggested, should be purchasing at least 250 volumes a year per thousand of the population, and at least 90 of these should be adult non-fiction. For an independent library service the minimum annual acquisitions should be 7200 volumes, in certain specified categories, with at least 50 periodicals and up-to-date editions of basic works of reference.

The second working party report, on *Inter-Library Cooperation in England and Wales* (1962), was concerned with the regional library bureaux and the National Central Library, and its recommendations will be dealt with below.

The outcome of all these deliberations was the important Public Libraries and Museums Act of 1964, which came into force on 1st April 1965, superseding all previous library legislation. The Act required every library authority to provide 'a comprehensive and

137. THE COUNTY LIBRARIES
The county library service was now making rapid strides, but for a long time centres and branches still had to be accommodated in makeshift premises. These three pictures from Kent County Library show (*above opposite*) a library centre in a private house at Ivychurch; (*below opposite*) a branch in a converted shop at Petts Wood; and (*above*) exterior view of the Sandwich Branch, also in a converted shop.

efficient service', and in order to facilitate this, and to clarify earlier legislation, authorities were now specifically empowered to collaborate with each other; to create joint authorities; to provide pictures, gramophone records, films, and other non-book materials; to use their premises for educational and cultural activities and to make a charge therefor; and to make a charge for book reservations, overdue books, catalogues, and other special services.

In the much disputed matter of the optimum size of library authorities the Act left a good deal of discretion in the hands of the Secretary of State for Education, upon whom the duty was laid 'to superintend and promote the improvement of the public library service'. Parish library authorities disappeared, but all other existing authorities were allowed to continue, subject only to the provision that non-county boroughs and urban districts of less than 40,000 population might be deprived of their powers if the Secretary of State deemed that this would result in an improvement in library

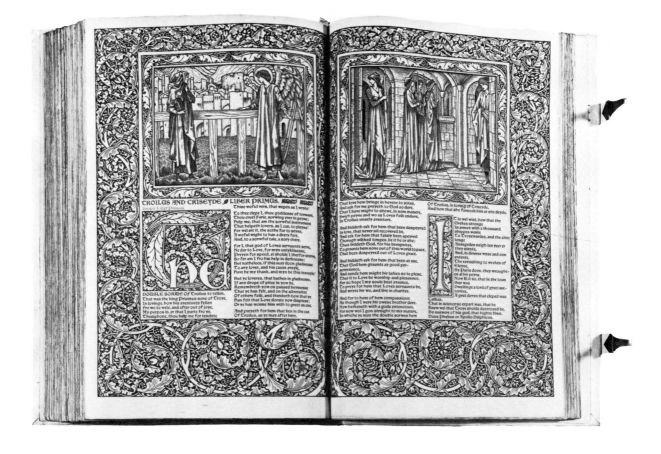

facilities. Non-county boroughs and urban districts seeking library
powers must have a population over 40,000.

The Secretary of State was also empowered to prescribe arrangements for inter-library cooperation and to designate regions for this
purpose. He was to be assisted in the task of supervision by two
Library Advisory Councils, one for England and one for Wales.

The Roberts Report and the two working party reports that
followed it represented a major advance in thinking about the
organisation and standards of the public library service, and there is
no doubt that if the 1964 Act could have been fully implemented it
would have gone a long way towards eliminating the smaller and less
efficient library authorities that had been the bane of the service for
so long. Unfortunately the Act had hardly come into force when the
government was once again forced to impose severe restrictions on
local government expenditure, and this made it impossible for the
Department of Education and Science to insist too strictly on the
officially prescribed standards.

Some progress was indeed made. Even before the Act, many
authorities threatened with the loss of their library powers increased
their expenditure in the hope of preserving their independence.
Others decided to give up the struggle and surrendered their powers
to their respective counties. Some of the county authorities merged
with neighbours – the Isle of Ely with Cambridgeshire, the Soke of
Peterborough with Huntingdonshire. In Scotland similar trends were
observable. The 1964 Act did not apply in that country, but a working
party report on *Standards for the Public Library Service in Scotland*,
published by the Scottish Education Department in 1969, made
recommendations comparable with those made south of the Border.

In the end, however, it was not library legislation but local government reform that brought the battle of the boundaries to an end. Many
of the smaller units of local government inherited from the nineteenth century – municipal boroughs, urban districts, rural districts
and parishes in England and Wales, burghs and parishes in Scotland –
were, in the mid-twentieth century, as inefficient for local government
purposes generally as they were for library administration, and the
possibility of reform had long been in the air. A beginning was made

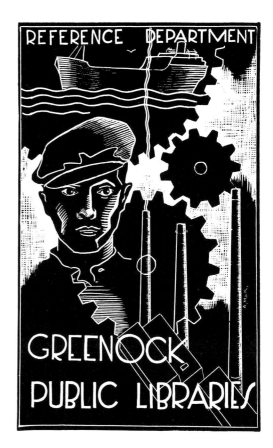

139. SOME MODERN
LIBRARY
BOOKPLATES
From left to right
Wigan, by L. T.
Howells, 1933;
Greenock, by A. S.
Mackenzie, 1940;
Liverpool, by
Stephen Gooden,
1943;
Leeds, by Kenneth
Lindley, 1959

with the London Government Act of 1963, which came into force in 1965, on the same day as the Public Libraries and Museums Act. This reduced the 29 authorities of London proper to 13 – the City of London and the 12 Inner London Boroughs. The 40 authorities of Greater London, with parts of the counties of Hertfordshire, Essex, Surrey and Kent, and the whole of the county of Middlesex, were grouped into 20 Outer London Boroughs. Library administration was correspondingly simplified, but even allowing for this, and for the disappearance of the parish libraries and the voluntary surrender of powers by some smaller libraries, there still remained, at the beginning of 1974, close on 400 library authorities in England and Wales and over 80 in Scotland.

The major reform in England and Wales was brought about, after much controversy, by the Local Government Act of 1972, which came into operation on 1st April 1974. Under this Act England and Wales outside London were divided into 6 metropolitan counties – Greater Manchester, Merseyside, South Yorkshire, Tyneside, West Midlands and West Yorkshire – and 44 non-metropolitan counties. The metropolitan counties were divided into metropolitan districts – 36 in all – which were self-governing except for certain

CITY OF LIVERPOOL
PUBLIC LIBRARIES

PRINT ROOM & ART LIBRARY
Incorporating the Agnes & Norman Lupton Bequest

overriding powers exercised by their respective county authorities. Only the metropolitan districts, and the non-metropolitan counties, might function as library authorities, except that in Wales, which comprised 8 counties, a county district might establish a right to library powers (four districts in South Wales were in fact approved for this purpose). The Local Government (Scotland) Act of 1973 brought about a similar consolidation of local government areas. With effect from 16th May 1975, the country was divided into 9 regions (each sub-divided into districts) and three island areas (Orkney, Shetland, and the Western Isles). Three of the regions (Highlands, Borders, and Dumfries and Galloway) and the three islands areas, were library authorities; in the remaining six regions library powers were vested not in the regional authorities but in the 37 district authorities, giving a total of 43 library authorities for the whole of Scotland.

The net result of all these local government changes was that the number of library authorities was reduced from a total of 465 to 163. McColvin, it may be remembered, had proposed 93 authorities, so the new arrangements were much less drastic, especially in Scotland. Their implementation was none the less a traumatic experience for the senior library staff involved. Many a chief librarian found himself prematurely pensioned off, or serving as deputy to a former colleague, or even serving as a district librarian in the library where he had once presided in proud independence. One of the saddest changes was the break-up of the splendid West Riding County Library, which found itself divided among the new authorities of North Yorkshire, Cleveland and Lancashire. In the main, however, the process of reform in England and Wales involved consolidation rather than division. Most of the new authorities were serving populations in excess of 200,000, and this meant larger resources and more widespread and more effective use of specialist staff and equipment. It was an advantage, too, that the boundaries of most of the English and Welsh library authorities now for the first time coincided with those of the education authorities, a fact which opened up the possibility of fruitful collaboration in a whole range of educational and cultural activities. However painful the transition, therefore, it is to be expected that local government reform will eventually operate to the benefit of the library service.

In Scotland the outlook is less favourable. One clause in the Local Government (Scotland) Act of 1973 does indeed impose on each local authority a duty 'to secure the provision of adequate library facilities' for all persons resident in its area. This requirement is parallel to that imposed on library authorities in England and Wales by the Public Libraries and Museums Act of 1964, but Scotland still has no equivalent Act. The decision to give library powers to the districts, moreover, means the dismemberment of Lanarkshire and other large county authorities, and the consequent destruction of the long-standing county link between the public libraries and education. In spite of the overall reduction in the number of library authorities, therefore, many people look to the future with grave misgiving.

Completing the National Structure

The supervisory role of the Department of Education and Science, as defined by the 1964 Act in respect of England and Wales, was of crucial importance in the new national library structure, and was reinforced when in 1966 a government Rate-Support Grant Order indicated that library expenditure would in future qualify for grant in aid. Many times in the past librarians had campaigned for central government assistance, but the proposal had always been rejected, often with pious protestations about the need for preserving local independence. It was, therefore, ironical that the change should have been effected simply by administrative fiat, without debate and almost without comment.

The position of the Scottish Education Department in relation to libraries is much less clearly defined, though the Library Cooperation Committee which now operates under the aegis of the National Library of Scotland fulfils many of the functions which in England and Wales are the responsibility of the Library Advisory Councils. Prior to the coming into force of the new Local Government Act in 1975 only the county libraries, which functioned as part of the educational system, were eligible for rate-support grant.

One of the duties laid on the Department of Education and Science by the 1964 Act was to define regions and prescribe arrangements for inter-library cooperation. The inter-library lending system established between the wars had proved, as McColvin had pointed out, cumbersome and inefficient, but in the postwar years a considerable streamlining was achieved, thanks largely to the inauguration in 1950 of the British National Bibliography, which at last provided a central cataloguing service for British publications. This was of great assistance to local libraries in their cataloguing work, and also facilitated the identification of books for inter-library lending. From 1959 it was agreed that each region should be self-sufficient in current British material, and an inter-regional subject specialisation scheme was introduced to ensure that no such material should be missed. These arrangements greatly reduced the burden of union cataloguing, and meant that the National Central Library could henceforth concentrate on older material and foreign literature.

In Scotland the Act of 1955 provided for statutory contributions from library authorities towards the cost of the Scottish Central Library, which had two years earlier absorbed the Scottish Regional Library Bureau. The Roberts Report suggested that in England and Wales there should be a compulsory levy on library authorities towards the maintenance both of the regional bureaux and of the National Central Library, and the working party on Inter-Library Cooperation subsequently appointed proposed that the number of regions should be reduced to four or five. Some librarians indeed took McColvin's view that the regional bureaux should be abolished, and all loans dealt with on a national basis. Following the 1964 Act the Department of Education and Science did not immediately exercise its new powers, preferring to await the outcome of local government reform, but the view gradually began to emerge that whatever the future pattern might be there would be a continuing role for the regions in local interlending.

To put the coping stone on the new national system, it remained to bring the local libraries into a more effective and organic relationship with the great national collections. In order to do this, however, it was first necessary to bring the national libraries into a proper relationship with each other. At the outset of the Second World War, as we have noted in an earlier chapter, these libraries were eight in number. There were to begin with the three great national reference libraries – the British Museum Library in London, the National Library of Scotland in Edinburgh, and the National Library of Wales in Aberystwyth. London also had three specialist libraries – at the Science Museum, at the Victoria and Albert Museum, and at the Patent Office. These also were primarily reference collections, though the Science Museum Library also provided a valuable lending service, mainly to institutions. Finally there were the two national lending libraries – the National Central Library and the Scottish Central Library.

In the postwar years the demands of science and technology became increasingly pressing, and in 1962, following a recommendation of the Advisory Council on Scientific Policy, a new National Lending Library for Science and Technology was inaugurated. This was in many ways an unusual library. Housed not in a great city but in the Yorkshire village of Boston Spa, and headed by one who was trained in science as well as librarianship, Dr D. J. Urquhart, it was designed specifically to provide a speedy service in scientific literature (especially periodical literature) not to individuals but to institutions – industrial and commercial concerns, research organisations, universities, colleges, hospitals, public libraries. Unconventional features included the shelving of books by title instead of by subject and author, and the use of an overhead cradle conveyor for transporting books and information. The system worked, and by 1965 the library was already handling as many loans as the National Central Library and the regional bureaux together.

One purpose of this new institution was to relieve pressure on the Science Museum Library, which helped to provide the initial stock. On the reference side the provision for science was strengthened by the creation in 1966 of the National Reference Library of Science and Invention, based on the former Patent Office Library. This new library operated under the aegis of the British Museum Library, though for the time being it had to be housed elsewhere.

The three national reference libraries all suffered, in the postwar years, from a desperate shortage of accommodation. In Edinburgh the opening of the long delayed new building for the National

Opposite:
140. NEW IDEAS AT BOSTON SPA
Above left Sorting book requests prior to transmission by cradle conveyor to the appropriate bookstack. *British Library*
Above right The item requested is placed on the cradle conveyor. *British Library*
Below The conveyor discharge and packing bay. *British Library*

141. READING ROOM AT THE SCIENCE REFERENCE LIBRARY, HOLBORN
The Holborn Branch of the Science Reference Library is the former Patent Office
Library. Another branch, at Bayswater, is specially strong in literature on the life
sciences and in scientific literature in the Slavonic and Oriental languages.
British Library

Library of Scotland in 1956 brought substantial relief, and in Aberystwyth the National Library of Wales also acquired additional accommodation in the 'fifties and 'sixties, but at the British Museum, in spite of all efforts to increase the available shelf space, the position became steadily worse. A new building was essential, and in 1964 plans were made public for an imaginative redevelopment of a site in Bloomsbury immediately opposite the existing library, but the use of this site gave rise to controversy, and in 1967 the government appointed a special Committee under the chairmanship of Dr F. S. Dainton (later Sir Fred Dainton) to re-examine the whole question of the national libraries.

The Dainton Report, presented in 1969, led to revolutionary changes in the organisation of the national libraries. These changes were set forth in a government White Paper of 1971, and the necessary legislative changes were embodied in the British Library Act of 1972. The major existing national libraries (other than the National Libraries of Wales and Scotland) were brought together in a single

142. THE NATIONAL LIBRARY OF SCOTLAND As early as 1928 Sir Alexander Grant made a gift of £100,000 towards the cost of this building, but it was still incomplete when in 1940 the Second World War brought operations to a halt. It was eventually opened only in 1956, and within a few years it was already too small. Originally designed by Reginald Fairlie, it was brought to completion by A. R. Conlon. *British Library*

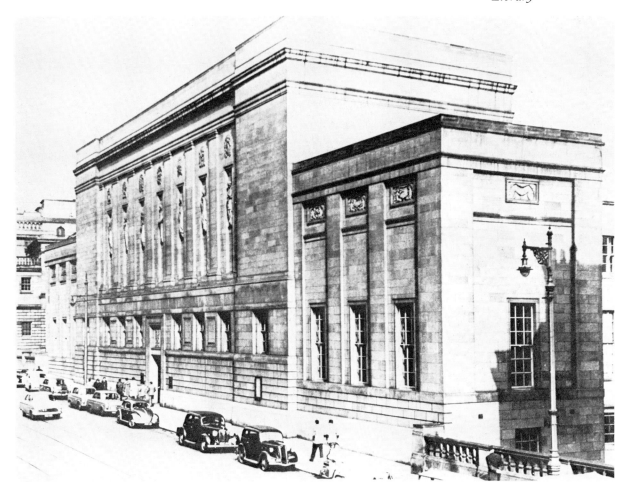

organisation known as the British Library, with three main divisions. The Reference Division was to comprise the former British Museum Library and the former National Reference Library of Science and Invention (now to be renamed the Science Reference Library). As soon as possible these libraries were to be rehoused on the Bloomsbury site. The Bibliographic Services Division, based on the former British National Bibliography and incorporating also the Copyright Receipt Office, was also to be centred in London, with the crucial role of providing catalogues and other bibliographical aids for the library service as a whole. The Lending Division was to comprise the former National Lending Library for Science and Technology, and the former National Central Library, and was to be located at Boston Spa. It was to provide a loan or photocopying service over the whole range of published literature for libraries and information centres throughout the United Kingdom, calling on the services of other libraries when it was unable to meet requests from its own holdings. The new system was brought into operation on 1 July 1973, and within two months the whole of the National Central Library's 750,000 volumes had been safely transported, by road and rail, to their new home in Yorkshire.

The National Library of Wales, the National Library of Scotland, the Science Museum Library, and the Victoria and Albert Museum

143. THE BRITISH LIBRARY LENDING DIVISION AT BOSTON SPA
A range of long low buildings for the most part (the site was originally an ordnance factory). The tall building recently erected to provide for the vast new intake from the National Central Library is prominent on the right.
British Library

Library were left outside the formal structure of the British Library, but it was envisaged that increasingly close working relations would be established with these and other specialist collections. The Science Museum Library, apart from its role in providing for the needs of museum staff, was to be developed as a reference library on the history of science and technology. In 1974 the Scottish Central Library was absorbed into the National Library of Scotland, becoming the Lending Services section of the Readers' Services Division. This change created in Scotland an organisation parallel in some respects to the British Library, though without the large lending stocks available at Boston Spa.

All these administrative changes, so tedious to describe but so immensely important, have created for the first time a comprehensive and rationally organised system of reference and lending libraries at the national level, serving as libraries of last resort not only for the public library system, with which in this volume we are primarily concerned, but also for the libraries of all kinds of other organisations which have in the past participated in regional and national cooperative schemes – universities, polytechnics, colleges, research organisations, and industrial and commercial concerns.

144. THE TREE OF KNOWLEDGE A Bewick engraving used in the bookplate of the Newcastle Reference Library. This bookplate was introduced after the presentation of the Bewick Collection to the library in 1904, and is still used for rare and valuable books. *Newcastle upon Tyne Libraries*

Further Reading

The developments described in this chapter can best be followed up in the official reports concerned. These are: L. R. McColvin, *The Public Library System of Great Britain* (Library Association 1942); C. S. Minto, *Public Library Services in the North of Scotland* (Scottish Library Association, Edinburgh 1948); Scottish Education Department, Advisory Council on Education in Scotland, *Libraries, Museums and Art Galleries: a Report* [McClelland Report] (Cmd. 8229, Edinburgh 1951); Ministry of Education, *The Structure of the Public Library Service in England and Wales* [Roberts Report] (Cmnd. 660, 1959); Ministry of Education, *Standards of Public Library Service in England and Wales* [Bourdillon Report] (1962); Ministry of Education, *Inter-Library Co-operation in England and Wales* [Baker Report] (1962); Scottish Education Department, *Standards for the Public Library Service in Scotland* [Robertson Report] (Edinburgh 1969); Department of Education and Science, *Report of the National Libraries Committee* [Dainton Report] (Cmnd. 4028, 1969); Department of Education and Science, *The British Library* (1971).

On inter-library co-operation see also P. H. Sewell, *The Regional Library Systems* (Library Association 1950, 2nd edn. 1956, Addendum in *Library Association Record*, Vol. LXI (1959), pp. 254–7; and R. F. Vollans, *Library Co-operation in Great Britain: Report of a Survey of the National Central Library and the Regional Library Bureaux* (National Central Library 1952).

Libraries in the Service of the Community

A Changing World

The progress of public libraries, like that of education, has been spasmodic and at times infuriatingly slow, but if we compare the position today with that at the beginning of the century we see that the progress has been very real. In making such a comparison we must recognise that the modern library exists in a quite different world. For ordinary people, thanks to the welfare legislation which followed the Second World War, it is a world of better opportunity and greater social security.

The advance in education has been particularly striking. In 1900 most people had to be content with an elementary schooling to the age of 14 or earlier. Secondary education was for a minority (probably less than 1 per cent), university education for a very small and privileged group indeed. Now, thanks largely to the Education Act of 1944 and subsequent developments, we have secondary education for all to the age of at least 16, and in addition a wide and varied provision for higher education. Taking into account not only the universities (almost doubled in number as a result of the Robbins Report of 1963), but also the colleges of education, the technical colleges, the colleges of further education, and the recently established polytechnics, the total number of full-time or sandwich course students in higher education in 1972–73 was 548,000, compared with 106,000 in 1945–46. Even this figure does not take into account Britain's latest and most spectacular venture in higher education, the Open University. This is a university specially for adult students, using radio, television, and correspondence courses to teach students working in their own homes in all parts of the country. Launched amid considerable scepticism in 1971, it had by 1973 already enrolled more than 40,000 students.

In spite of two world wars, and a seemingly endless series of political and economic crises, the development of science and technology has also brought a great increase in material prosperity. We see the signs of the affluent society all round us – in people's houses, their gardens, their motor-cars, their washing machines, their refrigerators, their television sets, their record players. Hours of work are shorter, holidays longer, and cheap 'package tours' have brought foreign holidays within reach even of quite modest incomes. Music, art, gardening, craftwork, sports and hobbies of all kinds have grown and multiplied. Paperback publishing, launched in its modern form with Allen Lane's Penguin Books in the mid 'thirties, has increased enormously since the war, and spread the habit of book-buying to new sectors of the population.

Much has been said, and more could be said, regarding the weaknesses of our modern social order, but there can be little doubt that it has resulted in a richer and fuller life for the great majority of people. As far as public libraries are concerned, these changes have been almost entirely beneficial. The extension of education, the development of technology, the growth of the welfare state, the growing complexity of central and local government, all these have brought fresh demands on the library service, and helped to create an atmosphere favourable to library growth. Even activities which appear to compete with library use, such as motoring, sports and hobbies, radio and television, are seen to generate new interests and new demands which are often reflected in increased library use.

A frightening feature of the current situation, and one which underlines the need for an efficient and economical library service, is the vast increase in the number of books published. In 1901 the number of books published in the United Kingdom was 6000; in 1938 it was 16,200; in 1973 it was 35,300 (including 9600 reprints and new editions). Fortunately in this matter, as we shall see, the advance of technology has come directly to the aid of the libraries: without the use of computers and other scientific techniques it would be impossible to maintain bibliographical control over this vast outpouring of material.

The Public Library Today

If we look, then, at the modern library, and try to compare it in imagination with the libraries of seventy-five years ago, the most obvious change is in the physical appearance of the buildings and the books. The late 'fifties and the 'sixties brought a quite unexampled spate of library building. Hundreds of new libraries were erected, and many older libraries were renovated and reconstructed. Most of the new buildings were urban or county branch libraries, built to serve new areas, or to replace buildings long out of date. The major

145. NEW LIBRARIES FOR OLD I

Above The Bebington Village Library, endowed by Joseph Mayer, a Liverpool jeweller, in 1866, and housed in a converted farmhouse. The Bebington Urban District took over control in 1930, but the original farmhouse still served as the central library until 1971.

Below Interior view of the new Bebington Central Library, opened in 1971: a typical modern open plan library.

British Library

Above Rhyd y Penau Branch Library, Cardiff, *c.* 1950.

Below The new branch, opened 1966. *South Glamorgan Libraries*

147. NEW LIBRARIES FOR OLD III
Above Queue to return books at entrance to Bradford Central Library, 1962.

Below Returned books and issue counter at the new Central Library opened 1967.
Bradford Libraries

148. NEW LIBRARIES FOR OLD IV
Above The original Buckinghamshire County Library Headquarters, 1923–54.
Below The new County Headquarters Library, opened 1966. *Buckinghamshire County Library*

One of the most impressive of the new library buildings, designed by Sir Basil Spence and opened in 1964. The library is the building in the foreground. *Times*

Below :

150. BIRMINGHAM CENTRAL LIBRARY

The most recent major library, officially opened in 1974. This great complex of buildings provides almost five acres of floor space and houses more than a million volumes. The reference library, accommodated mainly in the massive block at the rear of the picture, is the dominant feature, and is organised in eight subject departments. Provision is also made for a central lending library, a children's library, a music library (for books, records, tapes and cassettes) and a remarkable visual aids collection including more than 375,000 sheets of mounted illustrations in all subjects. The tower in the foreground of the picture is a memorial to Joseph Chamberlain.

Birmingham City Libraries

urban libraries were more difficult and expensive to replace, but there were some exceptions, notable examples being Norwich (1962), Hampstead (1964), Bradford (1967) and Birmingham (1973). A score or so of purpose-built county library headquarters buildings also made their appearance before building slowed down again at the end of the sixties. Such buildings, though designed mainly for storage and administration, usually made some provision also for readers in the immediate locality.

We still have some shabby and old-fashioned library buildings, but the newer buildings are light, airy and brightly coloured. Abandoning the Georgian and neo-classical styles which have so long been characteristic of civic buildings, they have experimented boldly with new shapes and new materials. Very often, following the postwar fashion in architecture, they are built on an open plan to allow maximum freedom of movement and maximum flexibility of use. The floors may well be carpeted, and the library may be adorned with occasional paintings or frescoes, or decorative arrangements of plants. Some walls may be almost wholly glass, to provide a 'shop window' on to the street. Except in the larger reference libraries, where much of the stock has to be held in reserve and asked for over the counter, there are no barriers to prevent the reader from wandering freely among the bookcases, which are normally low enough for all

152. JESMOND BRANCH LIBRARY, NEWCASTLE UPON TYNE
Quite a number of branch libraries have experimented with a circular or multi-angular plan. The library here shown, opened in 1963, was a pioneer in this respect. *Turners (Photography) Ltd.*

153. SWANAGE BRANCH, DORSET
In this county branch, opened in 1965, the use of glass walls provides a particularly effective 'shop window' at night. *Dorset County Library*

154. DORSET COUNTY
LIBRARY HEADQUARTERS,
DORCHESTER
County library headquarters
buildings nowadays often incorporate branch provision
for the local population. This
view of the entrance foyer
and display area shows an
effective use of a map of Old
Dorchester as a wall decoration. *Dorset County Library*

155. MURAL AT KIRKBY
BRANCH LIBRARY,
LANCASHIRE
In this county branch,
opened in 1964 (and now
part of the Metropolitan
Borough of Knowsley) a
large moulded fibre-glass
mural designed by W.
Mitchell is a prominent
feature of the decoration.
Lancashire Counties Libraries

156. FULHAM LIBRARY, HAMMERSMITH
Decorative plant arrangements are often, as here, an attractive feature of the modern library. *Hammersmith Public Libraries*

157. BARRHEAD BRANCH, RENFREWSHIRE
In this county branch, opened in 1960, one wall is adorned by a photomural of the Clyde Estuary. *Renfrew District Library*

158. EAGLESHAM BRANCH, RENFREWSHIRE

The 'browsing area' at this branch, opened in 1963, is designed for comfort and relaxation. Note the prints on the walls and the attractive furnishings. The ashtray would have horrified an older generation of librarians. *Eastwood District Library*

159. THE INTERNATIONAL LIBRARY, LIVERPOOL

Liverpool was a pioneer in the arrangement of its central library stock by subjects, bringing reference and lending material together on the same shelves. The International Library here shown was constructed in what was once a tiered lecture-theatre beneath the Picton Reading Room. *Liverpool City Libraries*

160. BRADFORD
CENTRAL LIBRARY
The new Bradford Central
Library, opened in 1967,
is also organised on a sub-
ject basis. The photograph
shows the Social Sciences
Library. *Bradford Libraries*

161. DISPLAY OF
TRAVEL BOOKS
AT MALVERN LIBRARY
Books themselves, since the
invention of the plastic
book-jacket, are part of the
decorative scheme, and a
great deal of trouble is
taken, as here, to arrange
attractive displays. Note
the upward tilted book-
cases, to make the books
easier to reach. *Hereford
and Worcester Libraries*

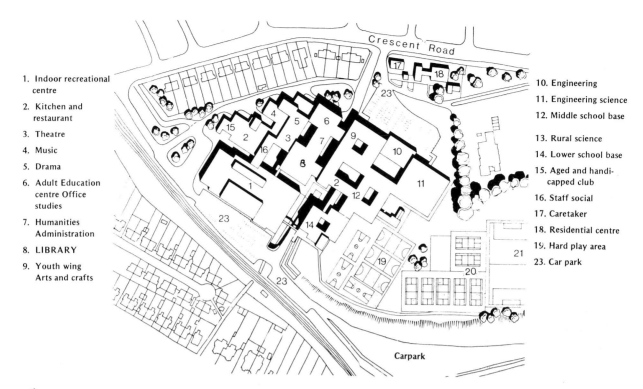

1. Indoor recreational centre
2. Kitchen and restaurant
3. Theatre
4. Music
5. Drama
6. Adult Education centre Office studies
7. Humanities Administration
8. LIBRARY
9. Youth wing Arts and crafts

10. Engineering
11. Engineering science
12. Middle school base
13. Rural science
14. Lower school base
15. Aged and handi-capped club
16. Staff social
17. Caretaker
18. Residential centre
19. Hard play area
23. Car park

162. THE ABRAHAM MOSS CENTRE, MANCHESTER The library stands at the centre of a great educational and recreational complex. *Manchester City Libraries*

the books to be within easy reach. Some large libraries, for example, Liverpool and Bradford, have abolished the distinction between reference and lending libraries, and made both reference and lending material available on open access, grouped according to subjects.

One of the striking changes is in the appearance of the books themselves, which once presented such a dismal appearance in their dark library bindings, but which are now, thanks to the invention of the plastic book cover, gaily displayed in their original jackets. This simple invention, which came into widespread use in this country only during the 1950s, did much to transform the appearance of public libraries, and incidentally halved library binding costs.

Much care and thought has gone into the design and location of libraries, bearing in mind such factors as the movement of population, the development of new housing estates, and the spread of car ownership. This last factor has led some people to think that a single large library, centrally placed and with ample parking facilities, would do the work hitherto done by a whole cluster of libraries, but a recent inquiry by the Department of Education and Science (*Public Libraries and their Use*, 1973), points out that such a policy penalises both children and old people, who are among the libraries' heaviest users. It recommends that wherever possible libraries should either be situated in a shopping centre or be associated with other community buildings. There have already been a number of experiments on these lines, an interesting example being the Abraham Moss Centre at Crumpsall, Manchester, in which the library forms part of a large complex of educational and leisure facilities.

The extent of library service is of course vastly greater than it used to be. Before the First World War it was restricted in the main to the towns, and even there, according to an estimate of 1907, only six per cent of the population were in membership. Now the service extends to every corner of the land – even to remote islands such as the Scillies and the Shetlands – and on the average a third or more of the population is taking advantage of it. In 1969–70 total bookstocks held by the rate-aided local libraries of Great Britain were in excess of 100 million volumes, of which about one-quarter were on loan at any one time. Main libraries and full-time branches numbered 2395; and there were 8262 part-time service points and 540 mobile libraries.

The growth of the county library service has been a spectacular feature of the postwar years. Even before the recent local government reorganisation major county libraries such as Essex and Lancashire were spending more on books than any of the great urban libraries. Increasingly, indeed, they found themselves being called upon to give an urban service, not only for commuters from the cities but for the inhabitants of the new towns, such as Crawley, Cwmbran and

163. MOBILE LIBRARY AT WANDSWORTH The large trailer library is particularly useful for work in urban and suburban areas. *G. C. Smith (Coachworks)*

164. MOBILE LIBRARY AT ROCKCLIFFE, KIRKCUDBRIGHT-SHIRE Smaller vehicles continue to meet the needs of isolated rural and seaside areas. *Edith Kelly*

Cumbernauld, created under the New Towns Act of 1947. Even in the rural areas, the old-style village centre has tended to disappear in recent years, giving way either to a part-time branch or to a mobile service based on a regional centre. Because of the large scale of their operations, and because, coming late into the field, they have not been saddled with old and out-of-date buildings, the county libraries have been better placed than many urban libraries to take advantage of new ideas and new techniques.

The mobile library now plays an important role in both urban and rural areas. In urban areas it is of special value in dealing with the problems created by shifting populations and the development of new housing estates. Some authorities use very large trailer libraries, which can be towed to a site and left for a whole day (or longer if necessary) without immobilising a motor vehicle. Such libraries can carry a stock of some 1500/3000 volumes. In the rural areas the mobile library provides a more efficient service than the part-time village centre, giving a wider choice of books and bringing the help of qualified librarians even to small hamlets and isolated farmsteads.

In the smaller islands of Orkney, where a mobile service is not practicable, the county library has since 1964 operated a 'Family Book Service' which makes use of the inter-island boat service. Each family may have, on request, a collection of 12–16 books which may be kept

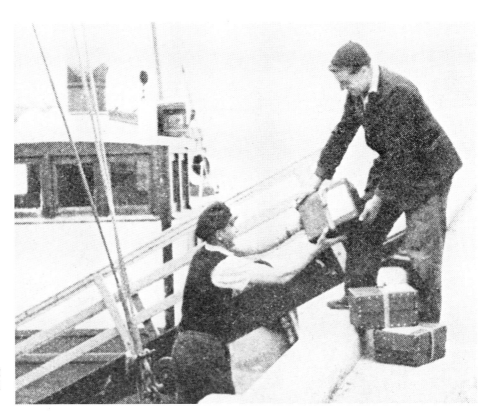

165. ORKNEY FAMILY BOOK SERVICE
Boxes of books being loaded on to a small inter-island boat.

up to two months. The books, packed in special boxes, are despatched twice weekly from the library headquarters at Orkney, and after being ferried over to the islands by boat are delivered by local traders' vans.

'Outreach' services of all kinds have been greatly extended. Many libraries are now providing, often with assistance from the Women's Royal Voluntary Service and other voluntary bodies, a special service to household readers – the elderly and the disabled – either personally or by bulk deliveries to homes and hostels. Provision for the blind is now made mainly by the National Library for the Blind, whose supply of Braille books is supplemented by the tapes made available by the British Talking Book Service for the Blind

166. SOME MOBILE LIBRARY USERS
Above left A Lancashire farmer. *Lancashire County Libraries*
Above right A Gloucestershire pensioner. *Gloucestershire County Library*
Below left A Scottish housewife. *Edith Kelly*
Below right A would-be reader of Watford. *Scammell Lorries*

(begun in 1935). Some public libraries assist in the provision of Braille books, however, and nearly all now provide large-print books for partially sighted readers.

Provision for hospital patients is still rather unsatisfactory, with the hospital authorities, the public libraries, the St John-Red Cross Hospital Library, and other voluntary bodies all involved, but the Library Association has done all it can to encourage the development of this work, and to train librarians to deal with its special problems. A considerable number of public libraries do in fact now provide a service to hospitals – some of them a very comprehensive service indeed, embracing not only a general lending library and reading room for all patients and staff (with a book-trolley service to patients in the wards) but also specialist provision in the way of books and periodicals for the medical staff. Though such libraries are inevitably small, they are managed by professional librarians and backed by all the resources of the public library concerned, including facilities for borrowing from other libraries where necessary.

In some hospitals experiments are going on in the provision of

books for the mentally ill and the mentally handicapped. Rampton Hospital in Nottinghamshire, for example, has a stock of 7000 books provided by the County Library – fiction, non-fiction, children's books and easy readers. It has also available on loan music cassettes, story cassettes, filmstrips and slides (and the apparatus needed for their use) and a library of over 400 toys, including games, jigsaws and musical instruments. Here, too, there is special library provision for the professional staff.

Other examples of special attention to the needs of 'extra-mural' groups may be seen in the Durham County branch library which operates within Durham Prison; in the Suffolk County branch library at the Hollesley Bay Borstal Institution; in the North Yorkshire County branch library in the Army Camp at Catterick; in the provision made by Devon County and other coastal authorities for service to shore-based lighthouses; and in the assistance given by the libraries at Glasgow and Cardiff in the provision of books for seamen.

168. SERVICE TO HOUSEBOUND READERS IN SEFTON Volunteers using their own cars provide service to old people's homes and individual housebound readers in Formby, Sefton. In some other parts of the library area the service is a provided by library staff. *Edith Kelly*

Library Use and Library Users

The old notion of the public library as mainly a working-class institution is now quite dead. The modern public library serves every class of the community, and indeed tends to be rather more middle-class than working-class. This emerged clearly from an extensive survey made in the London region in 1962–63, which revealed that the three highest socio-economic groups, covering professional, managerial and

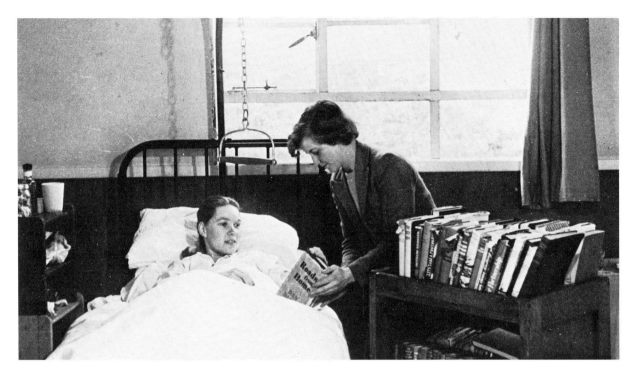

169. HOSPITAL
LIBRARY SERVICE I
Ward service by Kent
County Library at
Pembury Hospital.
British Library

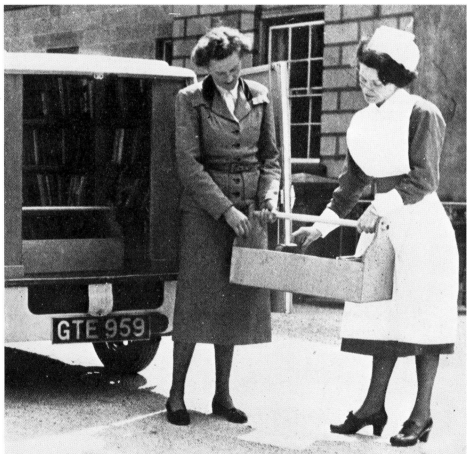

170. HOSPITAL
LIBRARY SERVICE II
Checking books for
ward service at Lan-
caster Moor Hospital
(a mental hospital),
by Lancashire County
Libraries. *Lancashire
County Libraries*

171. LIGHTHOUSE
SERVICE
A Devon County
Library delivery
driver exchanges a
box of books at the
Lynmouth Foreland
Lighthouse. *Devon
County Library*

executive occupations, accounted for 45·8 per cent of library membership, although these groups represented only 17 per cent of the total population. Conversely, at the other end of the scale, unskilled and semi-skilled workers were greatly underrepresented in library membership. In terms of absolute numbers, however, no particular social group is in a majority among library members.

Similar evidence has come from the provinces. The latest survey, included in a report on *Public Libraries and their Use* prepared by J. N. Taylor and I. M. Johnson for the Department of Education and Science (1973), covers libraries in the South Cheshire/North Staffordshire area and in the Lincoln area, and is concerned with actual library use as distinct from library membership. The two do not always coincide: for example library membership is about equally divided between men and women, but women tend to use libraries more. This survey did not attempt to categorise users in terms of social class, but it did reveal the rather striking fact that only one-third of library users were in paid employment. Housewives without other full-time employment accounted for a further quarter, students at school and university another quarter, and retired people one-eighth.

The figures for education tell a similar story. In the London survey 35 per cent of library members had stayed at school until at least 17 years of age. From the recent Government survey it appears that 41 per cent of library users aged 25 or over had stayed at school until at least 16 years of age. This still means, of course, that 59 per cent of users had left school at 15 or earlier, and had no further full-time education, and the proportion of older readers in this category was even higher: for those over 65 it rose to 73 per cent.

The increasing use of public libraries by the middle classes is an important social change, and is due to a number of factors. One, undoubtedly, has been the transformation, which we have already noted, in the physical appearance of the libraries themselves, and the books they hold. The modern public library, with its open plan, its carpets and pictures and 'browsing areas', and so on, often has a distinctly middle-class atmosphere, very different from the brown paint and scrubbed linoleum of the past. Another factor has been the virtual disappearance, by the early 'sixties, of the commercial circulating libraries, which found it impossible, in the face of rising book prices and the competition of cheap paperbacks, to maintain a satisfactory service. The oldest of them, Mudie's, had already disappeared in 1937, Boot's closed in 1966. The old 2d shop libraries, by this time commonly 4d or 6d libraries, faded out about the same time. The main factor, however, to which we shall have to return shortly, was the growing need of the middle classes for the kind of services that only public libraries could provide.

Some librarians have become worried lest the public library should become so middle-class that the less well educated reader would be afraid to use it. This concern is reflected in efforts, here and there, to assist in the campaign against illiteracy. This is a new development, for it is only recently that the country has become aware of the extent of the problem. It was long assumed that, since the 1870 Education Act, illiteracy had been virtually eliminated in this country, and it was a shock to discover that something like 4 per cent of the adult population, say about $1\frac{1}{2}$ million people, are either illiterate or semi-literate. The public library, of course, cannot take on the task of teaching them, but it can help with publicity schemes for literacy teaching, and by having available in appropriate branches an adequate supply of easy reading material suitable in content for the adult who has only just learnt to read. A number of libraries are now doing this, though there is still a shortage of texts suitable for this purpose.

Besides catering for all classes the public library now caters for all ages. In 1891, when Thomas Greenwood published the fourth edition of his *Public Libraries*, library users were commonly between fourteen and fifty. Children of school age were still generally excluded at that period, and older readers were both less numerous and less literate than they are today. The contrast with the present position is very striking. Special provision for children, supported, as we have seen in

172. A LIBRARY POSTER FOR BACKWARD READERS A design by Jan Baldwin, 1975. *New Library World*

the previous chapter, by all kinds of supplementary activities, is now an accepted and attractive feature of the library service everywhere. Even the toddlers are provided for, with special story-hours and 'browser boxes' of picture books. The big improvement in the quality of children's books in recent years has done much to increase the popularity of this branch of the service. As to the elderly, they are now amongst the most regular of library users. Indeed the recent Government survey on *Public Libraries and their Use* picks out the

**173. CHILDREN'S
LIBRARY AT
BRIERFIELD,
LANCASHIRE**
*Lancashire County
Libraries*

**174. BOOKS FOR
THE TODDLERS**
At the Hertfordshire
County Library
Stevenage Branch.
*Hertfordshire County
Library*

175. CHILDREN'S STORY HOUR AT LEYTONSTONE
The Children's Librarian reads a story in the Junior Study adjoining the Children's Library.
Central Office of Information

176. THE CHILDREN'S STORY HOUR ROOM
Some libraries now have specially equipped and decorated story rooms for children. This photograph was taken in 1968 at the Dunstable Area Library in Bedfordshire. *Bedfordshire County Library*

177. DRAMA FOR
CHILDREN
In the Children's
Library at a
Birmingham Branch.
West Midlands Press

178. THE EDINBURGH
LIBRARY CLUB
ANNUAL PICNIC,
1971. *Edinburgh City
Libraries*

179. SCHOOL
LIBRARY SERVICE
A Gloucestershire
County School Mo-
bile Library visits a
school at Lechlade,
1965. *Gloucestershire
County Library*

age-groups 5–14 and 65 and over as being those most likely to use the library service. Together they account for nearly one-third of all library users.

Close relationships have been established between libraries and schools, with most county libraries and an increasing number of urban libraries taking responsibility for the school library service. Local government reform, by making library authorities in most areas coterminous with education authorities, is bound to accelerate this development. Miss Lorna Paulin, County Librarian for Hertfordshire, writes on this subject (1972):

> For a long time a well-developed school library service has provided large collections of books for schools on long-term loan and supplemented these with special 'project collections' lent for a term or a year. Booklists have been prepared, permanent exhibitions maintained of books suitable for school libraries, travelling exhibitions organised, talks given, advisory visits made to schools, and courses have been run for teacher/librarians.

During the last few years all these services have been needed more than ever, and this aspect of the county libraries' work is one that has shown particularly rapid development.

Because so many pupils are now staying on to 18, secondary schools now require a wide range of adult books as well as books for children, and as more and more secondary schools become comprehensive it seems likely that the teacher/librarian will increasingly give way to the full-time professional.

One problem that worries many librarians is that of the adolescent who abandons the library as soon as he leaves school. A number of authorities, following the lead given by Walthamstow between the wars, have supplemented school provision at the secondary level with special collections of books for adolescents or 'young adults' in their own libraries, but efforts to enlist the interest of school leavers through library provision for youth clubs have not been very successful.

The large number of immigrants from foreign countries entering Britain since the war has posed a new problem for public libraries. Many of these immigrants have only a very imperfect knowledge of English, and if library facilities are to be provided for them it must be in their own language. The actual selection and purchase of books, however, is very difficult, since few libraries have staff qualified in the many different languages concerned. One way or another, however, the problem is being tackled. For Indian and Pakistani immigrants, who represent the main demand, there is now a central Loan Collection at the Birmingham Public Library, comprising books in Urdu, Hindi, Punjabi, Bengali and Gujerati; and a number of other libraries, especially in London, the Midlands, and the textile areas of Lancashire and Yorkshire, have their own small collections.

Other immigrants for whom special provision is made include Poles, who through their local libraries are able to draw on a loan collection established in London just after the war; and Greeks, for whose use a collection of literature in Modern Greek has been created at Camden Town.

A Threefold Task

It is time now to consider the actual functions which the library fulfils for these many and varied readers. These functions may be classified under three headings: recreation and culture; information; and education.

In spite of the fears expressed by our Victorian forefathers concerning the demoralising effect of too much fiction, the provision of recreational reading is now a normal and accepted part of a public

180. SOME LIBRARY USERS

This sequence of eight pictures taken in three Cheshire County Branch Libraries in 1975 illustrates the varied needs and tastes of those who use the ordinary county or suburban branch libraries. The users of the major urban reference libraries, of course, tend to be more concerned with professional and educational needs.

1

2

3

4

6

5

7

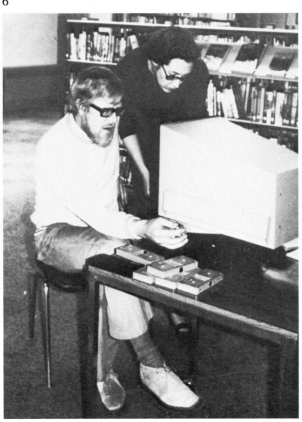

8

1 Most readers tend to look first at the new books on the returned book trolley.

2 Mr J. has sought the help of a member of the library staff in finding a good war story.

3 Mrs F. chooses a large print book for a friend who is partially sighted. In the next bay Mrs D. (with pram) is sampling a novel.

4 Mrs N. and her two sons are looking for a book on canals – a family interest.

5 Mr L. is looking for a guide to English pottery.

6 Mr R. seeks information on the 'solvay process' for making sodium carbonate. Assisted by a member of the library staff, he is consulting the library catalogue, which is computer produced and stored in microfilm cassettes. By turning the knob at his right hand he is able to bring the relevant portion of the catalogue before him on the microfilm screen.

7 Mr B., a commercial representative, is looking for a new job.

8 Mr and Mrs H. are consulting the *Family Guide to the Law* in search of help with a domestic problem.

library's work. It is, indeed, the dominant feature in most lending libraries, especially rural and suburban branch libraries. Much of the demand is for fiction of a fairly basic kind, and some libraries recognise this by allocating special shelves for the benefit of those who simply want a romance, a detective story or a 'western'. But there is also a demand, often it should be said from the same people, for works of a more general cultural kind – good modern and classical fiction, biography, history (especially local history), archaeology, travel, current affairs, natural history, astronomy, music, indeed all kinds of subjects. Figures published in 1963 for a single day's issues from the Liverpool Central Lending Library showed that in five out of seven subject groupings most of the issues were for 'non-professional use'. (The exceptions were the social sciences and technology.)

This wide spread of demand is in part a consequence of increased leisure, but it also undoubtedly reflects new cultural interests, awakened both by the extension of education and by the impact of radio and television. The serialisation of a novel on the media at once creates a demand for copies to read, and it is now generally recognised that, as the County Librarian of Renfrewshire reported in 1964, 'the more serious and informative television and radio programmes send a large proportion of viewers and listeners to books for further study'.

The informational function of the public library is concerned with those who are seeking an answer to a specific question, and has been increasing in importance in recent years as people more and more come to look upon the library as a community resource. Some libraries have established special information services with staff

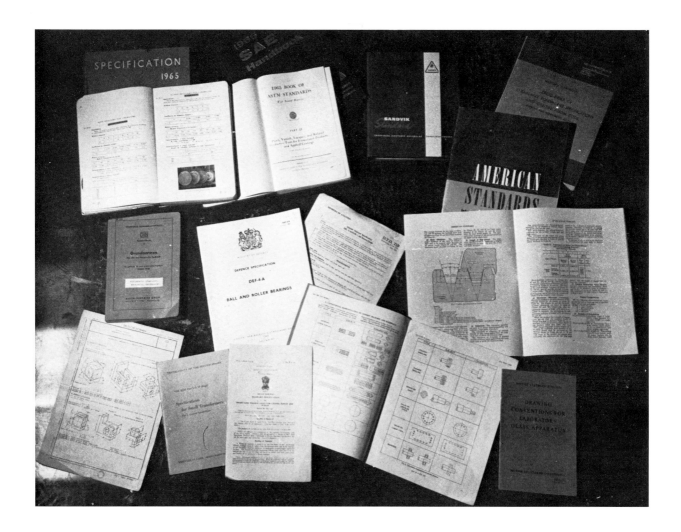

continuously engaged in compiling information and answering inquiries. Other libraries deal with such inquiries through their normal readers' advisory service. Many inquiries are concerned with local information, e.g. information concerning local officials, local amenities, local societies, local history. Others arise from domestic problems – pensions, social welfare, housing, investments, insurance, hire purchase, and so on. Furniture, antiques and other collectors' items bring many requests for information; so do gardening and other do-it-yourself activities; and there is a constant demand for information about holiday resorts. Many people also come in with quite specific inquiries. Questions recently received in the Central Library at Nottingham, for example, included in the course of a single day: Where is the nearest international airport to Amougies in Belgium? How can one identify Royal Copenhagen porcelain? What was the average wage in 1850? Who composed the ballet *Checkmate*? Where is Navy Island? What are the colours of the

181. BIRMINGHAM CENTRAL LIBRARY *Left opposite* A display of technical literature. *Left* A member of the staff answers an inquiry. *Birmingham City Libraries*

German flag? What patents have been filed in recent years for collapsible squash courts? and Which countries are the principal producers of charcoal?

Inquiries for commercial and industrial purposes are endless, and in the large central libraries are dealt with by special commercial and technical libraries, carrying a wide range of reference material: post office directories, telephone directories, trade directories for all countries, gazetteers, atlases, street maps, patent specifications, trade marks, information concerning currency, exchange and tariff regulations; and technical and trade journals from all over the world. Almost invariably these libraries are linked for this purpose with non-public libraries in their region – academic libraries, research libraries, industrial and commercial libraries – in cooperative schemes along the lines of the SINTO scheme developed at Sheffield between the wars.

As an example of the services given by such cooperative organisations we may cite the one based on the Liverpool City Libraries, which is known as LADSIRLAC (Liverpool and District Scientific Industrial and Research Library Advisory Council), and was formed in 1955 with support from the Liverpool Chamber of Commerce, the Merseyside Productivity Association, the Liverpool Trades Council, the Department of Scientific and Industrial Research, the Federation of British Industries, and many local firms. Its purpose is to assist local industrial and commercial concerns by providing the literature they need. It undertakes literature searches on request, lends books and documents from the libraries' own stock, and draws both on its own members and on a wide range of specialist libraries for material and information not available from stock. Photocopies of articles and documents can be supplied if required, and a technical information officer is available to visit firms and discuss their problems on the spot.

LADSIRLAC has available for immediate access the entire stock of the Liverpool City Libraries, embracing some two million books and several million documents. The Technical Library alone has some 100,000 volumes on open access, and currently receives over 1000 British and foreign periodicals. The Commercial and Social Sciences Library has a comparable collection; the Patent Library

183. KENT COUNTY LIBRARY HEADQUARTERS, MAIDSTONE— THE STUDENTS' ROOM, 1964
It is significant of the tremendous emphasis on educational needs that this county library should find it necessary to provide a special room for students in its new headquarters. *Kent County Library*

covers British and foreign patent specifications; the International Library has an extensive collection of foreign literature and maintains a register of translators. All British Government publications, and all publications of the major international organisations, are received as a matter of course. Periodical Technical and Commercial Bulletins provide classified lists of recent acquisitions of interest to members.

It is not necessary to spell out in detail the educational needs served by the public libraries today. The large expansion in secondary and higher education has already been noted, and its effects may be dramatically seen in the reference rooms of our large libraries, which are often full to overflowing with students from schools, universities, polytechnics, colleges of education, colleges of further education, adult education classes, and last but not least, the Open University. Most of these institutions have, of course, their own libraries, but the supply of books is never sufficient, and it is the public library that has to meet the unsatisfied demand.

The demand for what McColvin called 'purposive reading' (as distinct from recreational reading) is felt at all levels: even small branch libraries now need some kind of reference room. Inevitably, however, the demand falls most heavily on the major urban central libraries, many of which serve a regional as well as a purely local function. A survey of thirty-three public reference libraries in Great Britain (including all the major libraries) carried out by D. W. G. Clements in 1966, showed that 58 per cent of users were from the field of education, 18·9 per cent were from industry and commerce, and 11·3 per cent from central or local government or government subsidised organisations. The heavy educational use is very notable: in fact 52·6 per cent of all library users were students.

The range and variety of non-book provision has continued to increase. Music record collections, now available either free or at a small subscription at a number of libraries, are in the main a postwar innovation. The lead in this matter was taken by the London libraries.

185. AN OPEN ACCESS RECORD COLLECTION At the new Bradford Central Library, 1967. *Bradford Libraries* Inset 186. CHECKING THE STYLUS OF A RECORD-PLAYER The librarian must satisfy himself that the stylus used by the borrower will not damage the records. *Birmingham City Libraries*

Elsewhere, in view of the cost and the high risk of damage, libraries tended to hold back until after 1950, when the advent of the vinylite long-playing record greatly reduced the risk of breakages. Some libraries now also have music cassettes available on loan. The new branch library at Crumpsall, Manchester, is an example of a library offering both records and cassettes on loan. Members pay a subscription of a pound a year, and are entitled to borrow two items at a time (records or cassettes) for a period of four weeks. The collection includes both classical and non-classical music, the latter being divided into categories such as 'pop, progressive, soul, folk, jazz, standards, light music, and brass and military music'.

Another postwar development, so far only in a minority of libraries, is the loan of pictures. Holborn, in 1954, pioneered a scheme for the loan of original paintings by local artists. Loans were for a period of three months, at a charge of 10s, and the borrower had the option of buying the picture if he so wished, at a price not exceeding 20 guineas. Other libraries subsequently developed similar schemes, but not always for original paintings. Crumpsall, for example, has a free loan service for framed reproductions, which may be borrowed

187. NEGOTIATING A PICTURE LOAN
At the Holborn Central Library, 1961. The scheme has been continued by the present library authority, Camden.
British Library

for three months at a time. Colour slides are available to assist borrowers in their choice.

Services such as these are one aspect of the increasing involvement of public libraries in a great variety of cultural and educational activities. We have noted in the previous chapter the pioneering work of Edward Sydney of Leyton in this field before the Second World War. Swindon, a new library authority established only in 1943, shortly set a new pattern in library extension work by converting a redundant Sunday school into an Arts Centre under library control. The town's art gallery and museums were also brought into close association with the library, so that Harold Jolliffe, who became librarian in 1946, found himself directing a whole complex of cultural institutions. The library's own contribution, organised either directly or in collaboration with other bodies, included book weeks, exhibitions, concerts, theatrical performances, festivals, and adult education classes, besides a wide variety of activities under the auspices of sponsored societies.

A number of other libraries began to extend their cultural provision. The establishment of the Manchester Library Theatre (from 1951 under the management of the city librarian) is a striking example.

188. LIBRARY THEATRE AT THE LUTON CENTRAL LIBRARY *British Library*

189. CRUSH BAR
AT THE BRADFORD
CENTRAL LIBRARY
THEATRE
Bradford Libraries

The most remarkable development of recent years, however, has been the association of public libraries with local arts councils, which are able, through their Regional Arts Associations, to secure grants from the Arts Council of Great Britain for the support of music, drama and the visual arts. In 1970, in response to an inquiry, 33 libraries reported an involvement of this kind. In most cases the librarian himself either acted as secretary of the local arts council or was heavily involved in secretarial work: and invariably the library gave generous assistance, for example, by providing accommodation, publicity, and box office facilities. A number of new library complexes now include accommodation for exhibitions, concerts, and dramatic performances.

The London Borough of Camden is one of a number of London authorities which are playing an active role in the arts. A recent annual report included a record of six music recitals, two series of lunch-time record recitals, thirty-nine films, and six art exhibitions all arranged in Camden libraries during the year. In such activities we see the Kenyon Report's ideal of the library as the intellectual centre of the community taking practical shape. It is an ideal that was echoed in an address by Mr Denis Howell, a Parliamentary Under-Secretary at the Department of Education and Science, in 1967:

I still believe we need much more thought about the use of our

190. EXHIBITION ROOM AT BRADFORD CENTRAL LIBRARY *Bradford Libraries*

191. LOCAL HISTORY MUSEUM AT THURROCK CENTRAL LIBRARY
Essex County Library

192. ART
EXHIBITION FOR
CHILDREN
At Lancashire
County's Barrowford
Branch.
*Lancashire County
Library*

libraries – their social purpose. They ought not to be just book lending centres . . . In my view they should become cultural centres in the widest sense of that term – a place in which people can gather to talk, to hear a variety of discussions – the very heart of the local community.

Organisation and Staffing

Many of the larger public libraries, both urban and county, are now very big enterprises indeed, giving a varied and sophisticated service which makes full use of modern communication techniques. Telex is regularly used for the transmission of inquiries and book requests, both within individual library systems and in communicating with outside organisations. Microphotography in its various forms is used for the copying and storage of bulky material, such as newspaper files, and out of print material, such as nineteenth-century Parliamentary papers, which would otherwise only be available in other libraries. In many libraries microphotography is now used also for recording loans, a photographic record being made for each loan to identify the book, the reader and the date. This system is known as 'photocharging'. A less used variant is 'audiocharging', in which the particulars, instead of being photographed, are read by an assistant into a tape-recorder. Photocopying, and especially nowadays xerography, is extensively used both to increase stocks and to provide copies for use by readers: it is cheaper, for example, to send the reader a xerox copy of a periodical article than to arrange a postal loan of the actual periodical, especially if it is in bound form.

The use of computers, too, is steadily increasing, and as noted above is becoming essential to keep control of the flood of new material. Most libraries now rely, for their primary source of information on new British publications, on the British National Bibliography and other lists computer-produced by the Bibliographic Services Division of the British Library. The Division can also provide, if required, computer-produced catalogues tailored to the use of individual libraries. Local libraries which have their own computer, or access to a computer in another department, use it for stock control,

193. CHANGING METHODS OF RECORDING LOANS (I)
The traditional method, 'pocket charging' or 'card charging', in which an identifying card is transferred from a pocket in the book to a pocket in the reader's ticket, which is then retained by the library till the book is returned. This method, pioneered at Bradford in 1873, is still widely used. *British Library*

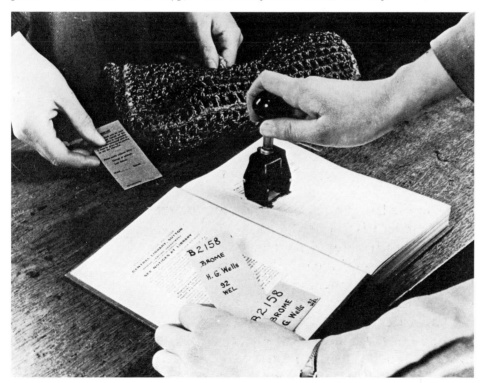

194. CHANGING METHODS OF RECORDING LOANS (II)
'Photocharging', a method first used in this country at Wandsworth in 1955. The assistant operates a microfilm camera which records at one operation particulars of the book, the reader's ticket, and the date. *Wandsworth Public Libraries*

for the control of ordering and accessioning processes, for the recording and control of book issues, and for the production of catalogues and booklists. Some libraries use a combination of techniques: Cheshire Libraries, for example, have a computer-produced catalogue recorded on microfilm and stored in cassettes for use in a microfilm reader. These and other new techniques are having a profound effect on library organisation, and are leading to a complete reassessment of many long accepted procedures.

Libraries both large and small make use of the interlending system. When a reader requests a book which is not in stock at the particular branch or other service point to which he applies, the first step is to

195. CHANGING METHODS OF RECORDING LOANS (III)
'Computer charging', the most recent innovation. The assistant uses a 'light pencil' to read specially coded details which are given on the book and on the reader's card. These particulars, with the date of the loan, are recorded on magnetic tape and stored in a computer. *British Library*

discover whether a copy is available at some other service-point in the same library system; if not, the request is passed to the regional library bureau, which searches its records to see whether a copy is available at some other library in the same region; if this fails, the request is passed to the British Library Lending Division at Boston Spa, which now deals with about three-quarters of all inter-library loans in the United Kingdom. The British Library can draw not only on its own stock, but on the resources of many other specialist libraries, including, as a last resort, even the great copyright libraries whose books are normally available only for reference. In special cases application is made to libraries abroad. In 1973–4 the BLLD

was able to satisfy 84 per cent of valid requests from its own stock, and a further 9 per cent from other libraries. Its own stock now amounts to $2\frac{1}{4}$ million volumes and over one million volumes in 'microform'; and it currently receives nearly 50,000 periodical publications.

Naturally libraries have been seeking ways of speeding up these interlending procedures. Large libraries, by special arrangement, are able to telex their needs direct to the BLLD without going through the regional library bureau. In the south-east, in 1969, the London and South-East Regions amalgamated, producing a powerful organisation known as LASER which operates with the help of computer-produced union catalogues supplied by the British Library Bibliographic Services Division. These catalogues list books by numbers, indicating for each book which libraries within the region hold copies. This makes it possible for a local library to arrange loans from other libraries directly without having to go through the regional bureau. The introduction in 1967 of a Standard Book Number for each book published greatly assisted developments of this

196. TREASURES OF THE BRITISH LIBRARY
The British Library Reference Division, in Great Russell Street (formerly the British Museum Library) has an immense store of bibliographical treasures both manuscript and printed, both Western and Oriental. Three famous examples are illustrated here: *Opposite left* Full-page picture of St Mark and his symbol, the lion, from the Lindisfarne Gospels, written and illuminated *c.* 700 A.D., probably in the island monastery of Lindisfarne.
Opposite right A page from an early fifteenth-century manuscript of Chaucer's *Canterbury Tales*, showing the beginning of the Merchant's Tale.
Left The title-page of the first and only volume of Sir Walter Raleigh's *History of the World*, written during his long imprisonment in the Tower of London, and published in 1614, four years before his execution. *British Library*

kind, making it possible to identify a book by number only. This system now operates on an international scale, and the letters ISBN, followed by a number, may now be found (printed on the back of the title-page) in the publications of many countries.

All too little has been said in this brief survey of library history about staff, but it must be clear that the developments which have been described call for a wide range of library staff, many of them highly qualified. Novelists and playwrights seem quite unaware of this change, and the old stereotype of the blinkered and bespectacled librarian, obsessed with the care of his books and ignorant of the world outside, still persists. It is doubtful whether this stereotype was ever more than a caricature: certainly it has no validity today.

Library staff today are either professional or non-professional. As far as possible the more routine duties – counter work, book processing, typing, packing and the like – are handled by non-professional staff whose training is basically clerical. The professional librarian, now known as a 'Chartered Librarian', must not only have a sound knowledge and training in bibliographical techniques and

197. BEHIND THE SCENES AT THE BRITISH LIBRARY
Above The Sorting Passage at the Reference Division, where books are sorted for dispatch to readers or return to the shelves.
Below Opening the day's intake of periodicals at the Copyright Receipt Office, formerly at the British Museum but now part of the Bibliographic Services Division in Malet Street nearby. *British Library*

198. LIBRARIANSHIP TRAINING
Books are still the librarian's main business, and the first of these three pictures from the College of Librarianship, Wales, shows a member of staff demonstrating the use of a manual printing press as a basis for exercises in conventional printing work.

There is however, in schools of librarianship everywhere, an increasing emphasis on audio-visual materials and on the use of audio-visual techniques for 'information retrieval'. The second picture shows the selection and editing of slides, and the third picture shows a demonstration in the computer laboratory of 'on-line' information retrieval, closed circuit television being used to show details of the keyboard and print-out. *College of Librarianship Wales*

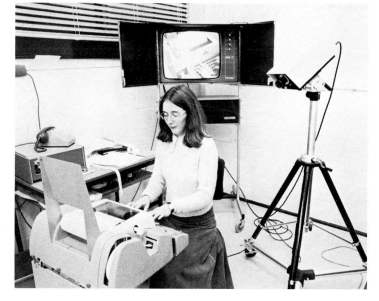

library organisation generally but must also have the more detailed knowledge and experience enabling him to specialise in some particular branch of library work, e.g. as a reference librarian, technical librarian, children's librarian, music librarian, local history librarian, or readers' adviser. If he (or perhaps we should say she, since three-quarters of library students are women) aspires to an executive post, it will also be necessary to have some training in management techniques, including, in these days, the basic technological concepts needed to cope with computers and other sophisticated equipment.

Until the Second World War, apart from the diploma course at University College, London, all training had to be part-time. After the war a number of technical colleges and colleges of commerce began to offer full-time two-year courses, and from 1964 this became the normal method of entry, leading to the Associateship of the Library Association (ALA). Those who seek a higher qualification may undertake research for the Fellowship of the Association (FLA). In the last ten years, however, an increasing number of students have preferred to take courses, either at a polytechnic or at a university, leading to a degree in librarianship, and some think this will be the pattern of the future. Professor W. L. Saunders of the University of Sheffield, writing in 1972, saw 'unmistakeable evidence that education for librarianship and information science is set on a course which must lead in time to an entirely graduate profession'.

There will, thank goodness, always be a place in our public libraries for the scholar and the bibliophile, but increasingly the need is for men and women who combine technical know-how with a wide knowledge of men and affairs, and a keen perception of social needs. It is upon these qualities that the community library service of the future will be built.

Further Reading

After the Second World War library literature of all kinds – books, periodicals, conference proceedings – proliferates and becomes increasingly technical, so that it is not easy to know what to recommend to the general reader. *The Year's Work in Librarianship*, published by the Library Association, continues to provide a useful guide up to 1950, with a single volume, exceptionally, covering the war years 1939–45. Since 1950 the annual survey has given place to a five-year survey. P. H. Sewell edited *Five Years' Work in Librarianship, 1951–1955* (1958), and subsequent volumes for 1956–60 (1963) and 1961–65 (1968). The latest volume in the series is H. A. Whatley (ed.), *British Librarianship and Information Science, 1966–1970* (1972).

For general library administration it is still possible to turn to J. D. Brown's *Manual of Library Economy*, of which a 6th edition, ed. W. C. B. Sayers, was published by Grafton in 1949, and a 7th edition, ed. R. N. Lock, in 1961; but it is advisable also to consult a more modern text, such as E. V. Corbett, *Introduction to Librarianship* (Clarke 1963, 2nd edn. 1966).

For special aspects of the library service the following can be recommended:

S. G. Berriman and K. C. Harrison, *British Public Library Buildings* (Deutsch 1966).

B. Groombridge, *The Londoner and his Library* (Research Institute for Consumer Affairs 1964); Bryan Luckham, *The Library in Society* (Library Association 1971); J. N. Taylor and I. M. Johnson, *Public Libraries and their Use* (Department of Education and Science 1973).

J. L. Hobbs, *Local History and the Library* (Deutsch 1962, 2nd edn. rev. G. A. Carter 1973).

Department of Education and Science, *The School Library* (H.M.S.O. 1967).

J. P. Lamb, *Commercial and Technical Libraries* (Allen and Unwin and the Library Association 1955).

M. E. Going (ed.), *Hospital Libraries and Work with the Disabled* (Library Association 1963, 2nd edn. 1973); B. M. Sanders, *Library Services in Hospitals* (Library Association 1966); D. Boorer, *The Mental Hospital Library* (Library Association 1967); M. J. Lewis, *Libraries for the Handicapped* (Library Association 1969).

R. F. Watson, *Prison Libraries* (Library Association 1951); Frances Banks, *Teach them to Live* (Parrish 1958).

Harold Jolliffe, *Public Library Extension Activities* (Library Association

1962, 2nd edn. 1968); Harold Jolliffe, *Arts Centre Adventure* (Swindon Borough Council 1968); Department of Education and Science, *Public Libraries and Cultural Activities* (H.M.S.O. 1975).

G. Bramley, *A History of Library Education* (Bingley 1969).

199. ECONOMY CAMPAIGN
A cartoonist's comment on the financial difficulties currently facing the public library service. *Punch*

"Sorry about War and Peace, dear, but the service could well be axed before you finish it."

Index